'N Sync
CONFIDENTIAL

ANGIE NICHOLS

Billboard

Created in 1999 by Virgin Books
an imprint of Virgin Publishing Ltd
Thames Wharf Studios
Rainville Road
London W6 9HT

First published in the United States in 1999 by Billboard Books, an imprint of
BPI Communications Inc., at 1515 Broadway, New York, NY 10036.

Library of Congress Cataloging-in-Publication Data for this title can be obtained from
the Library of Congress.
Library of Congress Catalog Number 99-61001
ISBN 0-8230-8353-5

Printed and bound in Italy by Graphicom

Designed by Stonecastle Graphics Ltd

First printing 1999

1 2 3 4 5 6 7 8 9/06 05 04 03 02 01 00 99

PICTURE CREDITS

ALL ACTION
61; John Mather 24; Nick Tansley 1, 4, 13, 19, 23, 29, 31, 47, 49, 55, 60, 68, 69, 70, 71, 73, 79, 80, 82, 83; Todd
Kaplan 56, 66, 67

CORBIS
Tibor Bozi 9

PICTORIAL PRESS
A.A. 3, 12, 16, 21, 26, 28, 50, 53, 63, 75, 78

REDFERNS
11, 14, 18, 22, 27, 34, 37, 46, 51, 52, 62, 76, 77, 86, 87; Jon Super 39, 44; Michael Linssen 15, 32, 57, 74, 85

SOUTH BEACH PHOTO AGENCY
Patrick G. Falcone 54; Pierre Zon Zon 17, 30, 36, 42, 65

STARFILE
Guy Wade 90; Jeffrey Mayer 41, 43, 89, 91; Jon Mead 6, 92, 96; Max Goldstein 33; Todd Kaplan 5, 10, 35, 58,
84, 95; Vinnie Zuffante 8, 38, 64

Contents

They're 'N Sync!

God must have spent a little more time on 'N Sync. Or if it wasn't exactly divine intervention that caused five singers from different parts of the US to become one of the hottest vocal groups around almost overnight, it must have been something very, very close.

How else to explain the success of 'N Sync, a group virtually unknown to music fans in 1997? Less than one year later, they saw their self-titled debut CD firmly installed at number two on the US *Billboard* album charts while simultaneously their collection of Christmas tunes, *Home For Christmas*, perched merrily at number seven. But that's not all. 'N Sync scored a hat trick when their first home video *'N The Mix* made its bow at number one on the *Billboard* video charts in the same month!

To cap a very happy season, 'N Sync won the award for Best New Artist at the 1998 American Music Awards beating Aussie "It" girl Natalie Imbruglia as well as alternative rockers Third Eye Blind. Voted on by a national sampling of 20,000 people from all across the country, the American Music Awards was the group's first important nomination and win. It was icing on the cake that they also scored two accolades from the *Billboard* Music Awards in 1998. Their video for "I Want You Back" scooped both the Best Clip of the Year award and the prize for Best New Artist Clip in the dance video category.

Not so bad for the group's first year in the big leagues, was it?

Despite their success, 'N Sync – JC Chasez, Lance Bass, Joey Fatone, Chris Kirkpatrick and Justin Timberlake – aren't really about awards, platinum records and industry plaudits. They're simply five young guys who want to make music from the heart. "Honestly, I didn't really think about it too much," JC told a room full of reporters when asked about 'N Sync's double success on the Top Ten album charts. "When we had the first album come out and it did so well, we were so happy. Then we decided to do a Christmas album – we never expected anything like this." The truth is that even if no one bought their records or handed them an award ever again, the members of 'N Sync would still be singing.

Part of the reason that fans of all ages have been irresistibly drawn to 'N Sync is the energy and enthusiasm they put into everything they do. Whether they're crooning a love song live on MTV or chatting on a morning talk show or standing in a crowded record store signing autographs for fans, JC, Justin, Joey, Lance and Chris always look like they're having a wonderful time. No matter where they go they're always laughing, joking and teasing one another. Although Chris is usually the instigator, all of the guys are masters of the art of the ironic comment and the sarcastic aside. Yet, the boys are so refreshingly honest, one can't help but laugh with them. After all, it's hard not to smile along with guys who are so clearly enjoying life and each other!

Much of the reason behind their obvious happiness is their genuine friendship. Unlike so many vocal bands, 'N Sync wasn't put together by a switched-on manager or record producer. With the exception of Mississippi-boy Lance, all the other members of 'N Sync knew one another long before they became members of the same musical team. Best of all, their shared experiences over the past few years have made Joey, JC, Justin, Chris and Lance even closer pals. After so much time on the road together, they can answer one another's interview questions with uncanny accuracy. What is even more unusual is that they still like each other. Their manager Johnny Wright has quipped that he's never, ever seen them argue. That scares him!

"We all have our differences of opinion but we're the best of friends," Chris explained. The most frequent topics the group has disagreements over are hairstyles, clothing and who gets to talk to an attractive girl first! As his flirty reputation suggests, Joey often wins this contest hands down! Fortunately, the other guys are not the kind to hold a grudge. "When there's a problem, we might clash but we'll always talk it over," Chris said. "None of us goes to bed angry. None of us goes on stage angry, we'll talk it over first."

While the world is full of entertainers who call their co-stars "brothers" as a publicity sound bite, there's no faking it with 'N Sync. For proof, the guys note that when they're home on

"I think our goal is to make the next album better than the first one…We're going to work really hard on that."

holiday they still call each other to get together for a night on the town! 'N Sync is one of the few groups whose members are sometimes together 24 hours a day, seven days a week and yet still enjoy being together – even in their spare time. They finish one another's sentences, laugh at one another's jokes and behave more like best friends than co-workers.

If their wildly hectic first year in the public eye has got the guys of 'N Sync pining for a holiday on their own and away from it all, they're not letting on. Rather than take a rest after the constant touring and promotion of 1998, 'N Sync actually picked up the pace for 1999. The guys launched a new string of concert dates with a New Year's Day show at the Thomas & Mack Center in Las Vegas, Nevada. It was followed by ten more shows in locations as far flung as Berkeley, California, Biloxi, Mississippi and lots of places in between.

February found 'N Sync back in the recording studio putting together songs for their third release, tentatively scheduled to appear in August or September 1999. "I think our goal is to make the next album better than the first one," Lance said. "We're going to work really hard on that." Using both new and familiar producers, the group sought to create another collection of diverse songs to attract the broadest possible audience. "It will be basically like the first format – very diverse, very different – so that it appeals to everyone," he explained.

The members of 'N Sync, who all contributed melodies, lyrics and vocal arrangements to their first two CDs, also expect to have more input into the most recent collection of songs to bear their name. "This record will definitely have a couple more songs written by 'N Sync," JC promised, adding that all the members of the group have been noting down bits and pieces when inspiration strikes. But the third album's release is just a small part of the plans that 'N Sync are drawing up to take the group into the next millennium.

What should fans expect? "Well, I'd tell you, but then I'd have to kill you," joked Justin with a sly grin at a press conference for the group. But seriously, 'N Sync plans include a new world tour, a possible live video, more television appearances and plenty of opportunities for the boys to get to meet their many fans. The boys are also considering an 'N Sync television series, and we might even see *'N Sync: The Movie*. Whatever the future holds, there's no doubt that 'N Sync are here to stay!

Justin Timberlake
The Cute One

Though he's the youngest member of the group, Justin Timberlake isn't the kind of guy to just sit back and let everyone else in 'N Sync make the decisions for him. Fully one-fifth of the 'N Sync vote and often one of its most vocal members, Justin knows what he wants and he isn't afraid to express his opinions. He's never been the kind of person to let his age get in the way of his dreams!

He's always been that way. For Justin Randall Timberlake, who was born on 31 January 1981 in Memphis, Tennessee, a career in entertainment was always a foregone conclusion. Justin's mother recalls that he always showed an aptitude for music. As a baby, he used to keep the beat effortlessly with his tiny foot in time to songs he heard playing around the house. Justin started singing just as soon as he could talk. By the age of two-and-a-half, she said, he was able to harmonize along with the radio.

A gift for music runs in Justin's family. His father, Randy Timberlake, has a wonderful voice. He sang and played the double bass in a bluegrass band with his brother in the early 1980s. Watching his father and uncle play on stage fascinated little Justin. When he was eight, he used to follow his dad around with a tiny plastic guitar that he used to hold backwards to imitate his father's bass playing.

Although Justin's parents, Randy and Lynn, split up when he was a schoolboy, he still considers his childhood to have been a happy one. Today when he's home in Orlando, Florida, he lives with his mother – his stepfather, Paul Harless, is a bank executive who flies in from Memphis to be with his family at weekends.

Justin also stays in close touch with his father and stepmother Lisa. In fact, they were present in Orlando when 'N Sync filmed their first concert for The Disney Channel. Justin is a very loving older brother to his half-brothers, Jonathan, who's five, and Steven, who will celebrate his first birthday on 28 August 1999. When they're together, Justin and Jonathan shoot basketball hoops or sing together. 'N Sync's most popular member proudly notes that little Jonathan has a good voice and dances well. Who knows? Maybe someday in the future fans will get a peek at 'N Sync: The Next Generation! Justin confesses that he never realized how much of a "family man" he was until 'N Sync started taking him away from his parents and younger brothers for months at a time!

Justin considers his own vocal training to have begun in church. His paternal family – his grandmother, father, uncle and aunts – had a long tradition of singing in the church choir. When Justin turned eight, he took his place among his family members and learned what it was like to sing as part of a group in front of an audience. He loved it immediately, appreciating both the spiritual uplift that music brings as well as the attention he got from the congregation.

Justin still believes very strongly in music's ability to touch listeners' souls. The 'N Sync song he likes best remains "(God Must Have Spent) A Little More Time On You", because of its gospel-tinted chorus and pure sentiment. This closet romantic has confessed that he thinks this song is a "classy" way of telling

someone exactly how special she is! Justin calls it "the perfect" love song!

Recognizing his raw but substantial talents, Lynn enrolled eight-year-old Justin in singing lessons after school. His classes led to more opportunities to perform. As a youngster, Justin sang in school musicals and talent shows. One year, he and a bunch of school friends even dressed up as then-teen sensations New Kids On The Block to perform a lip sync to their hit "Please Don't Go Girl" for a school assembly. Justin sang lead doing an able impersonation of New Kid Joey McIntyre.

Their act was such a huge success that they were asked to repeat their performance at another school, where their performance actually led to girls chasing Justin and company through the school's hallways as if they were real pop stars. Who could predict that just about five years later Justin would be the genuine article, or that a former member of the New Kids On The Block team would manage his famous group?

But Justin's dreams as a child didn't extend that far. He was thrilled to sing in choir, go to school and play basketball, his other obsession. In fact, Justin gets one of his nicknames, Bounce, from his love of the sport. As a child he often said that he wanted to grow up either to be a basketball superstar, like Michael Jordan, or a singer. Although Justin has fulfilled one of his wishes, he still has a dream of playing in the NBA (the US professional basketball league) one day!

Opportunity Knocks

When Justin was eleven, the syndicated TV series *Star Search* came to Memphis looking to book amateur talent for its show. Justin auditioned by performing a country-and-western song. The producers liked the curly blond-haired boy so much that they invited Justin and his mother to come to Orlando, Florida, to appear on the show.

Justin didn't win the top prize on *Star Search* – his performance earned him three and a half stars which was topped

by a little girl who sang a Broadway musical show tune. However, Justin ended up getting something far more valuable than first prize. By a lucky chance, *Star Search* filmed its show on the same Buena Vista Television studio lot as the *Mickey Mouse Club* (or *MMC* as longtime fans know it). Justin, who often watched the variety series on TV at home, learned that the show's producers were planning nationwide open auditions to cast new members. Better still, the *MMC* people were scheduled to visit Nashville, Tennessee. Justin could hardly contain his excitement! He and his mother flew home to Memphis, turned straight around and headed for the *MMC* auditions in Nashville.

In 1993, *MMC* auditioned some 30,000 children across the United States and Canada between the ages of nine and sixteen to fill seven spots in the cast. Twelve-year-old Justin Timberlake was one of the chosen few! Though the job entailed moving to Florida and changing schools, Justin has often said it was one of the smartest choices he's made in his life.

In the two years he spent as part of *MMC*, Justin learned volumes about singing, dancing, acting and performing before a live audience. Today, he credits the show with giving him a little bit of training in many different areas of the entertainment business. He performed music in many different styles – from country to rock to rap and R&B. He even got a chance to meet some of his musical idols who guest-starred on the show, such as Boyz II Men. Acting and performing in comedy scenes was a lot of fun, too. He's often said that he wouldn't mind acting in a comedy again some day in the future!

Justin still believes very strongly in music's ability to touch listeners' souls.

One of Justin's frequent partners in crime during his *MMC* days was JC Chasez, who was often called upon to act or sing with him in the same sequences. Despite a five-year difference in their ages, the pair found that they shared a love of basketball, a silly sense of fun and a complete dedication to their careers. The boys even shared a geographic tie as Tennessee-native Justin and Maryland-born JC both considered themselves sons of the South.

After *MMC* was cancelled in 1994, Justin and JC remained in touch. Justin resumed his high school career in Memphis while JC looked for work behind the scenes in the music industry. But Justin grew bored with the life of a normal kid. He is the sort of guy with bags of energy who has difficulty sitting still. He's always bouncing a basketball, drumming on a table with his fingers or searching for some sort of direction for his creative energies. It's not surprising that the life of an ordinary school student didn't hold much interest for him after his two-year brush with fame on the *Mickey Mouse Club*.

When JC visited Memphis, the guys planned some time together. They recorded some demo songs and briefly considered trying to find a recording contract as a duo. During that time, Justin introduced JC to his mentor, the vocal coach who would eventually bring Lance Bass into the 'N Sync fold. But that's getting ahead of the story.

Justin also explored the idea of pursuing a career as a solo artist. He and his mother moved back to Orlando in Florida, where he laid down some preliminary vocal tracks. Just as he was setting the wheels in motion for a record deal of his own, he received a fateful phone call from Chris Kirkpatrick, who was forming a new vocal group.

Justin and mother Lynn embraced the new project with open arms. For 14-year-old Justin, it was the opportunity to do something he loved with his closest friends – he was the one who brought JC into the mix. Lynn, meanwhile, was able to put her domestic and managerial skills to good use. For almost two years, she shared a house with Justin, Chris and JC, went on tour with them, advised them on business matters and even coined the group's name.

Although it might be hard for some mothers and sons to work so closely together, that was never the case for Lynn and Justin. They share a rare mutual respect for one another's opinions and experience. As for the other boys in the group, they'll always owe Lynn a debut of gratitude for doing so much for them, from

helping publicize 'N Sync and advising them on business matters to sewing up tears in costumes during the group's first shows.

'N Sync turned out to be a dream come true for both mother and son. Now that Justin is old enough to travel alone, his mother has built on her experience with the boys to develop a new career of her own. Her Florida-based management company, named Just-In Time Management after her famous son, handles the new girl vocal group Innocence, which features another former *MMC* cast member among its ranks, Nikki DeLoach.

For Fun!

Justin truly enjoys his life on the road with 'N Sync. Though he misses his family and keeps in constant touch with them by telephone, there's no place he'd rather be. For Justin, every night that 'N Sync is performing is a party.

When 'N Sync was starting out, the boys sang along to pre-recorded music. Today, 'N Sync travels with its own five-piece live band. Justin loves the spontaneity that performing with a live band allows. No two 'N Sync shows are ever alike! "The tempo might be faster one time or they can add something or we can stop the band if we want to do something else," he said. "It's much cooler." Though Justin enjoys the other aspects of the job as well – working in the recording studio, interviews, TV appearances and the rest – for him the greatest joy in the world is getting up on stage and performing for a crowd of cheering fans. Clearly for Justin, like so many other performers, basking in the appreciation of an elated audience is an addiction!

When he's not on stage or thinking about being on stage, Justin will probably be doing something athletic. This six-feet-tall teenager loves basketball and says that a really good game energizes him. While Chris and JC are also avid basketball players, they admit that Justin's height and devotion to the sport gives him a definite advantage when they battle it out one-on-one. Unless the weather is really awful, a day never passes without Justin shooting at least one round of hoops.

As a dedicated fan, Justin follows Michael Jordan's former team, the Chicago Bulls, and maintains a strong affection for the Orlando Magic. His sportsman's heart, however, belongs to the University of North Carolina's team. He follows all their games and frequently wears their blue team shirt.

Although he's never had to worry about his weight, Justin is very conscientious about going to the gym a few times a week to use the weights. He's not trying to become Arnold Schwarzenegger, but is instead working to build more visible definition in the muscles of his arms, legs and abdomen. He aspires to develop his abdominal muscles into a perfect "six-pack". Working out, he has said, also calms him down and allows him to focus.

What else does Justin like? Well, he has a passion for all things '70s – his room at home is a virtual shrine to the "have a nice day" decade, complete with candles and funky incense burners. He's also really into clothes. Designer Tommy Hilfiger is a recent choice of this blond-haired boy, who describes his style as a cross between sporty and hip-hop fashions. Like most guys his age, Justin also has a passion for designer footwear – Air Jordans, to be precise. Justin has a huge collection endorsed by his basketball hero. He even got his younger brother Jonathan into the act by giving him his own pair of Air Jordans for his last birthday in September. That's what older brothers are for!

On the personal side, Justin describes himself as a very private person who loves his family, respects his faith and enjoys the time he spends alone. Even when he's surrounded by his best friends in 'N Sync, Justin often withdraws into himself now and again. He can be found sitting in the back of the tour bus looking out of the window while his Walkman plays the sweet sounds of musical idols like Brian McKnight or Stevie Wonder. Later on, when he's recharged his batteries, he'll snap back into action by challenging one of the guys to a game of video basketball on the Sony PlayStation.

With so much going on in his life, Justin never has to worry about what he eats – he just pretty much fills up on whatever he likes. Given a choice, however, he'll usually pick healthy food. He loves carbohydrates – give him a bowl of pasta or cereal (especially the new Oreo O's breakfast cereal) and he's a happy man. Likewise, when he's thirsty, Justin reaches for a glass of milk, not because he's a health nut, just because he likes the

Justin jokes that he has millions of girlfriends all around the world these days, and it's not far from the truth!

taste. He once told a reporter that if he were trapped on a desert island, he'd take with him music, a spoon, a truckload of cereal and enough milk to eat it all!

Despite all the girls around the world who scream his name when he's up on stage, Justin doesn't really think he's that good looking. He's still learning to like his curly hair and moans that it's his least attractive feature. During his *MMC* years he used to try to straighten it, but now he's willing to live with his curls. Justin has also said that he is not comfortable about the way he looks in photographs. Sometimes when he's having his picture taken with the group and there are a lot of people watching he feels extremely self-conscious.

Justin jokes that he has millions of girlfriends all around the world these days, and it's not far from the truth! Many girls find him the most attractive member of 'N Sync. For his part, Justin first became interested in girls around the fifth or sixth grade at school. Although he'd had little crushes before, his first real

girlfriend lived right across the street. She initiated their first kiss one evening when she turned off all the lights as they watched television at her house. Unfortunately, the relationship didn't work out. When Justin took her on their first date to the cinema, she left him for another guy! Poor baby! He eventually recovered from the heartbreak.

Though Justin hasn't completely given up his dream of playing professional basketball with the NBA (he thinks he still could grow!), he's very happy with his life right now. Being a part of 'N Sync is a lifelong dream come true. While he has his moments of wishing he could be a normal schoolkid – going on dates, playing sports, sleeping in his own bed every night – he really wouldn't trade the challenges he faces today as a part of the group for anything in the world. His goal is to ensure the longevity of 'N Sync. "I think that's the goal for every artist," he commented to reporters at an 'N Sync press conference. "As long as we're moving ahead and upward, we'll be happy."

Justin's Confidential File

THE FACTS

* **Name:** Justin Randall Timberlake

* **Nicknames:** Baby, Curly, Shot, Bounce, Mr. Smooth

* **Birth Date:** 31 January 1981

* **Birthplace:** St. Jude Medical Center in Memphis, Tennessee

* **Hometown:** Orlando, Florida

* **Height and Weight:** 6ft tall, 160lb

* **Hair and Eyes:** Dark blond and blue

* **Parents:** Mother Lynn Harless and stepfather Paul and father Randy Timberlake and stepmother Lisa

* **Brothers:** Half-brothers Jonathan and Steven

* **Religion:** Baptist

* **Car:** Mercedes-Benz M Class in ruby red

* **Pet:** Ozzie, a Cairn terrier

* **Shoe Size:** 12 or 12$^1/_2$ – depending on the shoe

* **First Kiss:** Fifth grade

JUSTIN'S LOVES

★ **Music:** Stevie Wonder, Take 6, Dru Hill, Boyz II Men and Brian McKnight

★ **Actors:** Brad Pitt and Meg Ryan

★ **Films:** *12 Monkeys*, *The Usual Suspects* and *Ferris Bueller's Day Off*

★ **TV Shows:** *Seinfeld*

★ **Celebrity Crush:** Janet Jackson

★ **Food:** Pasta and dry cereal

★ **Drink:** Milk

★ **Hot Drink:** Tea

★ **Candy:** Runts and Sprees

★ **Ice Cream:** Daiquiri ice from Baskin Robbins

★ **Sport:** Basketball

★ **Basketball Teams:** Chicago Bulls and University of North Carolina

★ **Holiday:** Christmas

★ **Place To Visit:** Hawaii

★ **Memory:** Skiing with his family at Christmas

★ **Gift From A Fan:** A basketball

★ **Justin's Advice:** "You have to practice your craft if you want it to be the best it can be."

The Beginning

What's the recipe for creating the perfect male vocal group?

How do you guarantee to set female hearts pounding, capture

the covers of all the teen magazines and sell millions of records

around the world? In the summer of 1995, Chris Kirkpatrick

didn't have a clue!

H is only expectation when he brought together a bunch of his friends to form a new harmony group was that perhaps one day he'd be able to leave his job singing for the tourists at Universal Studios, Florida. At 24, Chris wasn't getting any younger. Although he enjoyed his stint performing with a doo-wop group called the Hollywood Hightones at Universal, he knew it wasn't his ticket to a more enduring career.

Today, when asked about how 'N Sync came together, Chris and the other guys have distilled their story of the group's evolution into just a few sentences. "I actually called up Justin who I met through his agent. These guys were on the *Mickey Mouse Club* and I'd worked with (Joey) at Universal so we were all kind of friends. We got Lance through Justin's vocal teacher. We were lucky in finding the right manager and the right business people. We got promoted from there and got a label and that's it!" said Chris, taking a breath.

Unfortunately, it wasn't quite that easy.

A Tale Of Two Theme Parks

Orlando, like most cities with a thriving entertainment community, is a very small town in some ways. Several studios have lots where films and television shows are produced. Two big rival theme parks, Walt Disney World and Universal Studios, employ hundreds of talented young singers and dancers. It has a vibrant music scene all its own and Miami is only a four-hour drive away. By the early 1990s, Orlando had quietly become the place to be if you were young, talented and looking for a big break into the music world.

Many of the performers who hung out on the Orlando audition circuit knew each other by face, if not by name. With the exception of Lance Bass, who joined the group later, the other members of 'N Sync had all met through being part of the Orlando arts scene. Chris and Joey Fatone became friends at Universal Studios where they both worked. Chris was introduced to Justin through an agent they both knew. Joey met JC because he had gone to Dr. Phillips High School with some of JC's former *Mickey Mouse Club* friends. And, of course, Justin and JC had performed together on *MMC*.

By August of 1995, the new group included Chris, Justin, Joey, JC, and a fifth friend, who eventually didn't work out. (In a stroke of strange irony, 'N Sync's lost member, who had been a friend of Chris since college, was also a dropout from that other hot Orlando group, Backstreet Boys!)

Each night the guys rehearsed their harmonies and dance steps in a large, empty warehouse they used as a studio. Though they didn't have a record label, a manager or even the promise of a gig, they took rehearsals very seriously. Practice often went on for four or five hours at a stretch with the guys dancing and singing the entire time. It was fun, but also very hard work because the warehouse had no air conditioning! At other odd hours of the day, the guys would get together to arrange their vocals and try out their harmonies.

One day while watching the group go through their routine, Justin's mother Lynn casually remarked how "in sync" their dancing and harmonies were. She thought that 'N Sync would be a perfect name for the new group. The phrase, she pointed out, was also a pretty close acronym using the last letter of each guy's first name. N was for Justin; S for Chris; Y as in Joey and C for JC. When Lance finally joined the group, the guys started calling him Lansten and the equation was complete.

When 'N Sync lost one of its original members, the boys tried to keep their group going as a foursome. For a time, Joey tried to sing the bass parts of their *a cappella* (without musical accompaniment) harmonies but it didn't come naturally to him. Their sound wasn't quite right. Needing another singer to be their "low guy," Justin turned to his vocal coach back in Memphis for a recommendation. Several phone calls, a plane flight from Mississippi to Florida, and one audition later – the guys sang "The Star Spangled Banner" together – and 'N Sync had found its final member in Lance Bass.

The first year was a struggle for the budding group. Joey and Chris were still working at Universal to play their rent and Lance was in the process of finishing his school exams through a correspondence course. Justin was still at school, too, while JC helped Justin's mother Lynn with the group's managerial duties. It all came together when, after months of rehearsals, 'N Sync felt the time was right to tell someone about their new group.

Something Special

'N Sync performed their first showcase at Walt Disney World's nightclub complex "Pleasure Island" in the autumn of 1995. That concert, filmed by a former *Mickey Mouse Club* cameraman as a gesture of friendship to JC and Justin, became the basis for the promotional video that 'N Sync sent to record and management companies. An entirely homemade effort, the video is now regarded by the members of 'N Sync as slightly embarrassing evidence of their early struggles. Still, it did work!

'N Sync picked the songs, the order in which they were performed, created their own choreography, designed costumes and even printed the posters to ensure that a crowd of friendly faces would be there for the show. That night, 'N Sync's fifteen-minute set included a bunch of original songs as well as a jazzed up version of the Beatles' classic, "We Can Work It Out."

In 1996, 'N Sync's promotional videotape attracted the attention of Backstreet Boys' business manager, Louis J. Pearlman. He passed the tape on to his right-hand man, Johnny Wright, former road manager of the 1980s pop phenomenon New Kids On The Block and then manager of Backstreet Boys. Although he had his doubts about taking on a second five-member harmony group, Johnny flew in from Germany to meet 'N Sync and assess their act.

Impressed by what he saw, Johnny put aside his reservations and immediately added 'N Sync to the line-up of Wright Stuff Management. He didn't take long to begin promoting his newest discovery to record companies around the world. Meanwhile, Johnny teamed the group up with proven powerhouse producers like the late Denniz Pop and Max Martin, who scored hits for Five, Robyn and Ace of Base, and Full Force, who had worked their magic on the Backstreet Boys. Before long, 'N Sync had a whole new repertoire of songs to rehearse.

Practice often went on for four or five hours at a stretch.

Later that year, 'N Sync released their debut CD on BMG Ariola Munich in Germany and Sweden. In an astounding turn of events the boys who'd been rehearsing in a warehouse only a year before, watched their singles "I Want You Back," and "Tearin' Up My Heart" become platinum-selling hits. But 'N Sync didn't have time to relax and enjoy their new fame. Johnny sent them on a worldwide tour that would take them not just through Sweden and Germany, but on to the UK, Europe, Asia, South Africa, Canada and Mexico, too.

Like Backstreet Boys before them, 'N Sync experienced the odd sensation of becoming famous abroad but remaining totally unknown in the place they called home! In a way, it was nice. Across Europe, the guys were chased through airports and staked out in their hotels. One German fan was so determined to meet 'N Sync that she actually hopped on the luggage belt in an effort to break through airport security and meet her pinups!

Back home in the United States, it was a completely different story. Justin, Joey, Chris, JC and Lance didn't attract any attention at all. They were able to do normal things like go to the cinema, a shopping mall or out to dinner without being noticed by anyone. While it was sort of nice, 'N Sync confess that it was also a bit of a letdown after all the excitement they attracted abroad.

Coming Home

That all changed in the spring of 1998 when 'N Sync released "I Want You Back" in the United States. Just as they'd done overseas, 'N Sync toured all the time, promoting their music on American radio stations, at shopping malls, county fairgrounds and just about anywhere else people would listen. It was exhausting work, but also satisfying because for the first time

their families and friends could see what all the fuss was about. "I think our friends are especially excited because they don't get to see what goes on over in Europe," Justin explained. "You tell them, 'Oh, I've got a number one album'. And they're like, 'Oh cool'. But here they can see it."

But 'N Sync's success in America didn't measure up to the mania they'd stirred up in Europe until they received an invitation from The Disney Channel to perform on a special *In Concert* show to be filmed at Walt Disney World theme park. Originally, the show was scheduled to star Backstreet Boys, but the older group was forced to back out at the last moment for personal reasons. 'N Sync stepped in to take their place. Filmed over the long Memorial Day weekend in May when America remembers its war dead, the show proved to be the perfect introduction to 'N Sync's music and the personalities in the group. It featured interviews with the boys, a live performance by 'N Sync at the Disney-MGM Studios, and irresistible footage of the guys and their families joking around and having fun as they rode the attractions at Walt Disney World's Animal Kingdom theme park.

'N Sync In Concert proved to be a powerful Cupid's Arrow that struck a lot of teenaged hearts when it was shown for the first time on 18 July 1998. It became one of the cable channel's most popular shows of the year and was repeated several times. Almost immediately, the group's popularity soared. New fans called radio stations requesting 'N Sync music, wrote to teen magazines begging for biographical information and bought lots and lots of CDs. The group's self-titled CD began to pick up a momentum on *Billboard's* album charts that never really slowed down that year.

To celebrate, 'N Sync doubled the pace of their promotional activities. Chris, Justin, JC, Joey and Lance appeared on morning talk shows, performed at more shopping malls and charity events and even braved a cold pelting rain to ride the M&M Mars float at New York's annual Thanksgiving Day Parade which was broadcast live on national television.

Opening up Janet Jackson's shows for a month in 1998 was an exceptional perk. 'N Sync was thrilled to receive the exposure of performing before sell-out audiences. Justin was also especially excited to meet Janet – the woman whose posters had hung in his bedroom when he was younger! Even the normally reserved JC couldn't help expressing his infatuation with the seductive singer. He said on MTV that he would have loved to trade places with the male dancer with whom she flirted at every performance.

On a break in Los Angeles, 'N Sync received full-out star treatment from *The Tonight Show with Jay Leno*. Lance explained that it had always been his dream to sit on *The Tonight Show's* couch and talk with Jay, a privilege rarely granted to the show's musical guests. The members of 'N Sync, however, were grateful to receive the invitation.

By the end of the year, the boys were presenting at the 1998 Billboard Music Awards (where they picked up two accolades themselves) and recording their second album release, *Home For Christmas*. 'N Sync also participated in a trilogy of Yuletide specials: *Holidays In Concert* for the Disney Channel, ABC's *Walt Disney World's Very Merry Christmas Parade*, and *Kathie Lee Christmas Everyday*.

'N Sync fans had no trouble figuring out which holiday played a special role in the lives of the group's members. "Everyone makes Christmas albums and the record company presented us with the opportunity so we snatched it up," explained Justin. He reasoned that only a group with a loyal fan base would ever be considered for such a project. It was great to be so highly regarded by their record company. "Also it's really a spiritual thing for us to celebrate Christmas. We did it basically just for fun."

Home For Christmas, a CD filled with both traditional and new holiday music, was released on 10 November 1998. Immediately, it took off, landing in the US *Billboard* Top Ten in its first week of release. On 18 November, 'N Sync enjoyed the spectacle of seeing their debut album *'N Sync* perch at number six in the US charts as their new Christmas album rested at an extremely awesome number seven. Clearly, all their hard work had paid off – big time! Their first home video, *'N The Mix*, and their

autobiography also rose to the top of their respective bestsellers lists. Clearly lots and lots of 'N Sync fans woke up on Christmas morning 1998 to find JC, Lance, Joey, Justin and Chris in one form or another smiling at them under their tree!

'N Sync was also earning respect in other areas of the industry. The producers of the holiday film *I'll Be Home For Christmas* snapped up one tune from their *Home For Christmas* CD. 'N Sync's "Under My Tree" appeared in both the film, which

starred former teen idol Jonathan Taylor Thomas, as well as the movie soundtrack. In addition, one of their songs from their debut album, "Giddy Up," found a home on the soundtrack of the *Sabrina, The Teenage Witch* series that year too.

Clearly, 1998 was an incredible year for 'N Sync. Surpassing their own dreams, they'd risen from obscurity to the top of the charts and commanded a loyal legion of devoted fans. Yet it was still only the beginning!

"It's really a spiritual thing for us to celebrate Christmas."

JC Chasez
The Serious One

Not many people can claim that they began their career in show business as the result of a dare, but that's exactly what 'N Sync's adorable JC Chasez did! Up until the time that this native of Maryland was twelve years old, he'd never sung or danced in public. He was far too shy!

Born on 8 August 1976 in Bowie, Maryland, not far from the US capital city of Washington, D.C., Joshua Scott Chasez is the oldest of three children born to Karen, a writer and editor, and Roy Chasez, a technician who networks computers at the White House for a living. JC's two younger siblings are Heather, now 20, and his brother, 17-year-old Tyler. Although both of them have done a few commercials, neither is serious about making a career in the entertainment industry at the moment.

The oddest thing is that until he turned 12, JC didn't know that he wanted to be in show business either. A fine student, who excelled at sports like American football and basketball, JC thought he'd like to become a carpenter or an engineer when he grew up because he was practical and enjoyed working with his hands.

However, as a child JC was always surrounded by good music. His mother encouraged her kids to appreciate a wide variety of music, including classical and jazz. At Christmas, the Chasez family would sing carols around the family tree. JC took his ability to sing in tune for granted and rarely used his gift for anything more than humming along with the radio. Singing was reserved for the shower!

A Friendly Dare

His perception of the world changed when JC entered his first talent competition because of a dare from a girl at school. JC wasn't there to sing though, he and his friend KC were urged to participate because of their dancing ability. "I used to go to clubs," JC explained. "This girl was like, 'If you dance with us in the show, we'll win for sure. I dare you, you're scared to do it.'" With the challenge thrown down and the promise that there would be lots of girls at the talent show, JC and KC agreed to participate in a three-minute dance routine set to MC Hammer's hit "U Can't Touch This." To everyone's surprise, their group won!

Newly confident about his abilities, JC entered more talent competitions in the Washington, D.C. area, and took first place in most of them. At thirteen, he started singing in contests, again, due to a dare! "[KC] dared me to go on stage and sing because I'd always be singing in his car," said JC. "He was like, 'I'll give you $20 if you go on stage and sing that song.'"

With the promise of enough cash for a couple of movie tickets, JC agreed to enter a talent competition singing the tune "Right Here Waiting" by pop star Richard Marx. It was a terrifying experience at first because all the other contestants were dressed up in formal clothes while JC was only wearing jeans. From the look of things, everyone else was taking the competition far more seriously than he was! However, once he got on stage and started to sing, the butterflies in his stomach settled down. Once again, JC took first place.

Around that time, his mother Karen (who calls her son "Josh" at home) noticed an ad in the local newspaper for a *Mickey Mouse Club* open audition. Despite his embarrassed protests, she

encouraged JC to try to get a place on the variety series. In 1991, the show's producers saw more than 20,000 kids during auditions for ten places on the show. JC is one of the few kids who made the cut!

During the four years he appeared on *MMC*, JC really blossomed. Days were spent singing, learning dances, acting in comedy skits and doing schoolwork. Surrounded by other cast members his own age, JC never felt that he missed out on a normal school social life like so many other people who entered the entertainment business as children. In fact, he's often said that going through those awkward teenage years was easier with so many good friends around. It was hard to feel bad about yourself when you were doing something so self-affirming and positive as a television show, he explained.

Today, JC keeps in touch with the friends he made during his years on *MMC*, many of whom are still in the entertainment field. Former *MMC* kid, Britney Spears, who recently had a hit of her own in the US on Jive Records with the song "...Baby One More Time," was invited by JC and Justin to open the show for 'N Sync during their first 1998 headlining tour. He also keeps in touch with Tony Lucca and Keri Russell. Like JC, this romantic duo is riding high today. Tony will be releasing his debut solo album this year, while Keri is the star of the hit Warner Brothers teenage drama *Felicity*.

JC wasn't just well-liked by his fellow *MMC* friends; he also became extremely popular with the show's viewers. By the final season of the show, he'd grown up into such a handsome guy that he received more fan mail than most of the other *MMC* kids.

His experience on *MMC* gave JC a chance to hone his singing voice. Fans of 'N Sync will have an easy time picking out his voice on the cast CD, entitled *MMC*, which was released in 1993. It's a very cute collection of songs showcasing the talents of the future 'N Sync star. Standout selections include JC singing the lead on the songs "Let's Get Together" and "I Saw Her First." He even got a chance to perform these songs live that summer when the

MMC gang travelled across the country on a promotional tour. It was JC's first chance to perform live for his fans and he really loved the experience.

During his four years on the show, JC also had plenty of chances to develop his acting skills. Though he played many different characters on *MMC*, none approached the popularity of Clarence "Wipeout" Adams, a clueless surfer dude who showed up frequently in comedy routines. Though music remained his first love, JC enjoyed the process of "bringing out different emotions" as an actor. If he had the chance to act again, and it wouldn't interfere with the progress of 'N Sync, he'd definitely give it another try.

After *MMC* came to its natural end in 1994, JC decided to continue his education in the ways of the music business. He moved to Los Angeles for a while to work with different writers and learn more about the crafting of songs. In Nashville, he sang on some demos and soaked up everything he could persuade people to tell him about the engineering and production processes. If the opportunity to join 'N Sync had not come along, he would have definitely pursued a solo singing career or teamed up with Justin as a musical duo.

"[KC] dared me to go on stage and sing because I'd always be singing in his car… He was like, 'I'll give you $20 if you go on stage and sing that song.'"

Obviously, JC has no regrets about joining 'N Sync. The successes the group has achieved in such a short time go way beyond anything he could have ever imagined himself. And although he had his first brush with stardom as a teenager on *MMC*, it did little to prepare him for the worldwide fame and devotion he has won from fans as a member of 'N Sync. "It's cool. You always want success but there was no way of predicting this much would happen to us," he said. "Obviously, I'm very happy with the current events that have transpired."

The busy schedule and constant activity of his life in 'N Sync perfectly suits JC's goal-oriented personality. An "all or nothing" kind of guy, JC would rather not do something if he can't devote enough time and energy to it to do it well. He's the most serious member of the group, the one most likely to call the others together to suggest that they get down to business. He's the member of the group most likely to go home early in anticipation of a busy day ahead. Unlike some, JC doesn't fool around in the recording studio or before a show. He's much too busy learning all he can from the producers, engineers, sound and lighting people. There's no part of the entertainment industry he doesn't find fascinating.

JC carries a set of keyboards with him wherever 'N Sync goes on tour. Not a day goes by without him playing them. The other

guys joke that since he purchased it last year, his personality has become his keyboard! When he's home, JC's dad Roy says he'll often spend whole afternoons bouncing back and forth between musical instruments – from piano to guitar to keyboards. JC has written some songs for 'N Sync and he hopes to see a lot more of the group's self-penned tunes on future CDs.

On His Own

Away from the spotlight, JC is considered the most sensitive and sentimental of the 'N Sync bunch. Though the other guys kid him, he really is a big fan of romantic comedies – especially ones starring Meg Ryan. He loves fantastic adventure, like the stuff in the *Indiana Jones* and *Star Wars* films, but he's not a fan of bloody and violent movies.

Though Joey has a reputation as the biggest flirt, JC wins the award for 'N Sync's biggest romantic. He's the member of the group most likely to quietly offer a girl he likes a single red rose. If she's really lucky, he might even read her a passage from one of Shakespeare's love sonnets or write her a song! JC has admitted to serenading a former special someone with a unique song written just for her.

However, like the rest of the guys in 'N Sync, JC is resigned to putting his love life on hold for the next three or four years. It wasn't an easy resolution for JC to make because he's always been very fond of the company of the fairer sex – and the feelings have been mutual! He admits he even went through a wild "girl crazy" phase when he was at school!

He met his very first girlfriend when he was only in nursery school. Her name was Lea Thompson and they held hands a lot! He was around six or seven years old when he received his first kiss from her.

JC went on his first real date when he was in seventh grade – around the age of 12. He took a girl he liked from school to a party. Romance blossomed as they danced all night together and never left one another's side.

On his own, JC would be content to wear a pair of boots, Levi's and a tee shirt all the time.

Not as showy, loud or aggressive as many guys, JC can actually be a little bit shy around people he doesn't know well! His ideal way to spend an evening off is just staying home with a stack of good films and a few dishes of take-away Chinese food. An old-fashioned kind of guy, JC prefers quiet dates at restaurants off the beaten path where he can give his dinner companion his undivided attention. He also enjoys going to plays, but he prefers dramas to musicals because he sees quite enough singing and dancing on stage with 'N Sync!

JC's best-loved hobby is sleeping. It's no exaggeration! With 4 a.m. wake-up calls to catch a plane and 1 a.m. bus rides down the world's motorways a frequent feature of 'N Sync's itinerary, the guys all operate in a constant state of sleep deprivation. It affects JC the most! After a month on the road he starts dreaming about an unbroken eight hours of sleep in his own bed.

Without realizing it, many of 'N Sync's fans have helped JC enjoy the shut-eye he so desperately misses. Since he never knows when the opportunity for a quick nap will arise – in the airport waiting room, on the bus, in a hotel lobby – JC often selects a couple of the plushest, softest stuffed animals that have been thrown on stage by fans to use as pillows! (The rest of the stuffed toys that don't go home with the group are usually donated to a local children's hospital.)

JC is cited as the most serious member of 'N Sync, who demonstrates the most perfectionist tendencies, but that doesn't mean he doesn't like to have fun. According to his dad, when he's home he'll spend hours in the backyard perfecting gymnastic flips and handstands. JC loves to suck on lollipops and he carries a yo-yo in his backpack everywhere he goes.

The main items that JC collects are Hard Rock Cafe menus. He's got more than 30 of them lining the walls of his room at home from countries such as Japan, Mexico, Malaysia, England and France. He once even talked a London Hard Rock waitress out of a menu pin she was wearing! Talk about an obsession.

Despite all the Hard Rock hamburgers and fries JC must eat in a typical year, he's extremely lucky that he's not the sort of person to put on weight. He's always been thin, a quality he really likes about himself because it allows him to wear just about any style of clothing.

On his own, JC would be content to wear a pair of boots, Levi's and a tee shirt all the time. Unlike Justin, he's not that in-the-know about designers or impressed by an expensive label. He likes clothes from Guess and Nike. Not a trendy sort of guy, JC prefers to wear a neat, slightly preppy look.

JC doesn't want to limit his future to being just a pop star. Although he absolutely loves his role in 'N Sync, there are so many other doors in the entertainment industry that he'd like to open. He'd love to become a top songwriter and producer. He'd like to learn more about the engineering process that goes into an album. He'd even like to manage a group of his own someday. JC also hasn't ruled out acting – he really enjoyed the skits he performed on *MMC*. With his handsome good looks, he could be a movie star! And, although it's a long way off, there's still that solo album waiting on his back burner. Wouldn't that be cool?

No matter where his personal road takes him, 'N Sync fans can be sure that there's nothing that JC will do that he won't pursue with his entire heart and soul. With such devotion, how can he not succeed?

JC's Confidential File

THE FACTS

* **Name:** Joshua Scott Chasez

* **Nickname:** Mr. Sleepy

* **Birth Date:** 8 August 1976

* **Birthplace:** Bowie, Maryland

* **Hometown:** Orlando, Florida

* **Height and Weight:** 5ft 10$\frac{1}{2}$in tall, 150lb

* **Hair and Eyes:** Dark brown and blue

* **Parents:** Roy and Karen Chasez

* **Brothers and Sisters:** Sister Heather and brother Tyler

* **Religion:** Christian

* **Car:** Black Jeep Cherokee Sport

* **Pet:** Grendal, a cat

* **Shoe Size:** 11

* **First Kiss:** Lea, aged seven

* **Unique Collection:** JC collects Hard Rock Cafe menus from around the world

JC'S LOVES

⭐ **Music:** Sting, Seal, Stevie Wonder, Brian McKnight, Boys II Men, Jodeci and Dru Hill

⭐ **Actors:** Harrison Ford, Mel Gibson, Tom Hanks, Julia Roberts, Meg Ryan, Halle Berry

⭐ **Films:** The *Indiana Jones* trilogy and all of the *Star Wars* movies

⭐ **TV Shows:** *South Park* and *Fresh Prince of Bel Air*

⭐ **Celebrity Crush:** Janet Jackson

⭐ **Food:** Chinese

⭐ **Drink:** Iced tea or water

⭐ **Hot Drink:** Tea

⭐ **Snack:** Tostitos chips with cheese dip

⭐ **Ice Cream:** Mint chocolate chip

⭐ **Sports:** Basketball and American football

⭐ **Sports Team:** Washington Redskins

⭐ **Book:** *The Hobbit* by J.R.R. Tolkien

⭐ **Clothing Brands:** Nike and Guess

⭐ **Place To Visit:** Colorado

⭐ **Gift From A Fan:** A fifteen-page poem

⭐ **JC's Advice:** "Treat people the way you want to be treated. If you give respect, you'll get respect."

In Concert

For fans of 'N Sync, there's nothing more exciting than experiencing their best-loved band at a live performance. It's more than just the thrill of hearing the songs you know by heart sung live.

An 'N Sync show is a one-night-only party with Justin, Joey, Lance, JC and Chris hosting the festivities. With dramatic lighting, awesome dancing and those fabulous voices, it's impossible not to feel like the star guest whatever seat in the house you may have.

The group humbly admits that their performances just keep getting better! In the early days, 'N Sync didn't have the clout to travel with their own live band so they sang and danced to recorded backing tracks – almost like performing with a karaoke machine! Though those early shows were lots of fun for the boys, they regretted that they couldn't be as free as they'd like because they had to use pre-recorded music. It didn't allow for as much interaction with their fans and didn't permit them to be as creative with the interpretation of their songs. Every night sounded pretty much like the night before.

These days, 'N Sync can have anything they want on tour. Their 1999 trip around the United States, topping the bill at arenas for the first time ever, was the most elaborate undertaking of their careers. In addition to a five-piece live band, the group added more costume changes, flashier special effects and large video screens so that even the fans in the back would get a great view. "It's a matter of maintaining a level. People have enjoyed our small show a lot. People have enjoyed the intimacy – that's the feedback that we get," said JC. "When we move to bigger

shows, we want to keep that sense of intimacy. That's what we have to work at. It's keeping a big room small."

With a larger budget and almost a guarantee of a sell-out every single night, the guys are able to use a much bigger stage with showier lighting and brilliant pyrotechnics. "It's really cool because the bigger the tours get, the more creative you can be and the more things that are in your reach," explained Chris. "So it's like the sky can be the limit the bigger we get."

Pre-Show Rituals

Whether the show takes place at an intimate 300-person club or at an arena which holds several thousand people, the guys from 'N Sync have a pre-show routine that rarely varies. On the afternoon of a performance, Lance, JC, Chris, Justin and Joey will arrive at the venue for a sound check. Usually, the band is there too. All the performers move about the stage to the different spots they'll be hitting during the actual show. Usually, there's no music, everyone just walks through the action so that the lighting, sound and special effects technicians can be sure that everything works as it should. Sometimes the sound check may only take half an hour, other times, when there is a problem it can hold everyone up for a whole afternoon.

After the sound check, the boys are free for a few hours. Sometimes they have appointments to do publicity at a radio station, magazine or record store; other times, they can choose to do a little shopping or go back to the hotel to rest. On some days, they might just hang out backstage and talk to the other people on their team – their tour manager Ibrahim Duarte, the band, security guards, management representatives, tour publicists, wardrobe mistress or whoever else is about. Although fans see 'N Sync as only five guys, there actually is a whole "family" of people behind the scenes whose job it is to ensure that each performance is as perfect as possible.

Even after all these years as a performer, he still makes a face when the time comes for him to sit in the chair! It's a pretty quick business though – the most the guys ever need is a bit of cover-up on any skin blemishes and some powder so their foreheads and noses won't shine under the hot stage lights.

Hairstyling takes a bit more time. Like most good-looking guys, the 'N Sync boys care a lot about their hair! Currently, Tigi hair products are the group's preference (except for Chris – he just washes his braids with a little dandruff shampoo and he's ready to go!). Tigi's Bed Head is a thick grooming wax that gives 'N Sync the sexy, mussed look that's so popular with their fans. Even Lance, who cares the least about his locks, thinks it's pretty cool. Still, he can't always be bothered – he usually just keeps his hair short, washes it with Finesse (his choice of shampoo because it makes his hair soft) and gets going.

The boys of 'N Sync are usually finished with hair and makeup in 30 to 45 minutes. Whatever remaining time they have left before they're scheduled to appear on stage is strictly "quiet time." Security keeps all guests away from the guys as they relax and clear their minds of everything but the coming show. The group's wardrobe assistants are also licensed masseuses, so if anyone is particularly tense or has a muscle ache, a pre-show massage can help ease away the strain.

Long ago, the guys decided that doing a round of hacky sack – kicking a little bean-bag ball around to each other in a circle – was a lucky 'N Sync pre-show ritual. It actually started as a joke. "We had to delay the show sometimes because we're not very good," recalled Lance with a laugh. Today, it's done more for fun than superstition. When 'N Sync opened up for Janet Jackson's Velvet Rope show during October 1998, the boys didn't have enough room to hacky sack backstage without disturbing others. They skipped that part of their pre-show routine to no ill effect. However, 'N Sync's hacky-sack circle was revived for their headlining 1998-1999 shows.

On the other hand, one pre-show ritual that the 'N Sync guys

Two or three hours before a show, the entire 'N Sync family eats together when caterers bring buffet-style food to the venue for dinner. It's a time for everyone – security team, technicians, management and performers – to have a bite together and relax before the night's show. Dinner isn't elaborate. There's usually salad, pasta or rice and two meat or chicken dishes to choose from along with bottled water, soft drinks or iced tea to wash it down. Dessert consists of slices of cake, some pudding and coffee or tea for anyone who wants it. Everyone serves themselves, sits where they want and enjoys a break from the intense work of putting on a cutting-edge show.

After dinner, Chris, Joey, Justin, Lance and JC move into the wardrobe area to change into their costumes and get their hair and makeup done. Although they are consummate professionals about it, the guys all dislike wearing makeup – especially Justin!

take very seriously is their prayer and group hug. No matter how rushed they are, they would never miss it. JC explains that it's more than a blessing, it's a way for their entire staff to bond before the show. "We give a prayer and a hug to everyone in our circle," he said. "We just make sure that whatever differences that anybody has had or if anyone's in a bad mood – it's squashed. It's time to be in sync with everybody. That includes management, that includes security, that includes everybody. We consider everyone who works with us our family. Basically, we give our family a hug before every show."

Then it's cue the lights, cue the band, cue the music – time to be really 'N Sync!

"We consider everyone who works with us our family."

In The Zone

'N Sync shows are an energetic blending of five distinct personalities, along with half-a-dozen hit songs, wild choreography and one madly cheering, thoroughly excited audience. Whether the show takes place in Albany, New York, or Madrid, Spain, it always is, as Justin would say, a "par-TAY"!

Part of the reason for that is the energy and enthusiasm of 'N Sync's fans, who in the group's opinion are the best fans in the world. Thanks to their success in so many different countries, the guys in the group have been able to compare 'N Sync fans' reactions all over the world.

American fans are extremely supportive of the group. They're enthusiastic about everything from a CD signing to an appearance on a talk show. They make the guys feel welcome wherever they roam. European fans like to follow the group everywhere when they visit their country. "It's a game," the 'N Sync boys explain, to know the group's whereabouts every moment of the day and night! 'N Sync fans in Spain are the most aggressive, say the guys, because they try to reach out and grab them! And Hawaii boasts the loudest concert fans that 'N Sync have ever heard!

One of the reasons for all the screaming is 'N Sync's exciting live show. In addition to the awe-inspiring vocals that the fans know and love from the group's CDs, 'N Sync's concert makes use of a lot of very intricate choreography. Chris has often cited 'N Sync's dance skills as one of the key differences between his group and all the other guy bands currently competing for attention. With the exception of two songs performed *a cappella*, 'N Sync dance through every song they perform in concert.

Over the years, the group has used at least three different choreographers – some whose résumés include work with Janet Jackson, Michael Jackson, the artist formerly known as Prince, and Usher. 'N Sync's members also contribute a lot of their own ideas for dance moves and combinations.

On their smaller club tour, 'N Sync started their show with the main theme from *Stars Wars* – not coincidentally, JC's choice as coolest movie of all time. The boys would all come out on stage wearing identical white jumpsuits with their faces shielded by shiny white helmets. As the crowd cheered and whooped, the guys performed an impressive robot dance to a funked-up version of the theme. Finally, with the audience whipped up into a frenzy, the guys' would remove their helmets and launch into one of their long-awaited hit songs like "I Want You Back."

40

After the first two songs, 'N Sync often perform the part of the show that Chris likes best. It's a tightly choreographed dance to an ever-changing array of popular Top 40 songs by other artists the group admires. Audience members are likely to see some of 'N Sync's famous acrobatics during this portion. On really good nights, all five guys will team up to do a back flip "in sync"! Sure, such stunts are a little dangerous, but the reaction they get from the fans is worth it.

As the crowd cheered and whooped, the guys performed an impressive robot dance.

Though the guys try to be extremely careful, accidents have happened. Chris remembers the time he did a flip but didn't make it over the whole way and landed on his head! It was more embarrassing than painful, he says. For Joey, his moment came when he landed badly and sprained his ankle during a concert. He finished the show in terrible pain, went backstage, removed his shoe and found that his toes had turned blue! And most famously, Justin's fall on a wet concert stage during an outdoor performance in Germany in 1997 resulted in a broken thumb! This brave guy also finished that performance before seeking treatment. Most of the time, however, 'N Sync's performances are flawless with each guy singing, dancing and jumping around in time to the wild screams of their fans.

The audience really does become a part of an 'N Sync concert. As well as encouraging the crowd to sing and dance along with the music, the boys sometimes compete for who can make the fans scream the loudest. Joey, Justin and Lance will ask one part of the audience to scream "IN," while JC and Chris will encourage the remaining fans to yell "Sync!" The energy the guys whip up in the arena is amazing! Other times, they get the kids in the crowd to chant, "Yes, yes, here we go, 'N Sync has got the flow." Beware! It's hard to leave an 'N Sync show without a very sore throat!

In addition to performing all their biggest hits – fans should expect to hear "Tearin' Up My Heart," "I Want You Back," and "(God Must Have Spent) A Little More Time On You" among others – 'N Sync often include a few songs made famous by other people. For a time, 'N Sync performed the 1950s hit "The Lion Sleeps Tonight," a song Chris used to sing when he worked at Universal Studios. They've also covered the Bee Gees' "Stayin' Alive," "Rock With You" by Michael Jackson and have performed a new version of Christopher Cross' 1980s hit "Sailing" which appears on 'N Sync's debut CD. The group also likes to include a brief set of current hip-hop hits by other artists with Justin acting as 'N Sync's human beat box. It's extremely cool!

What goes through the guys' minds as they stand up in the bright lights bathed in the devotion of their adoring fans? It's a little hard to explain. "Being on stage is like being in a different mind set from anything else you've ever experienced. It's like when you talk to an athlete and you ask them, 'What were you thinking?' They say 'I was in the zone.' It's like that," Justin has said. "I couldn't really explain the feeling of being out in front of 22,000 people. You can't explain the feeling. It mutes everything that you hear because it's so loud. The energy that flows is just incredible and really hard to explain."

Chris, another sports fan, has said that, like a professional athlete, the guys in the group need to work hard to flush all other thoughts from their minds and find their zone. "Sometimes you get on stage and you can feel that you're not exactly in the zone," he said. "So you have to go backstage during one of the breaks and try to focus as hard as you can to get in that zone."

Quick Getaway

After the last song but before the house lights come up, Chris, Lance, Justin, Joey and JC make a run for the exit. Not just the stage exit, they actually leave the building! Usually the boys have just enough time to grab a towel to dry off and a bottle of water before they dive into their bus, still wearing their stage clothes! There are never any wild parties backstage and no post-show autograph sessions for 'N Sync.

The group uses this "quick out" technique to discourage fans from waiting around inside and outside the venue in the hope of meeting their idols. If they waited until all the audience left their seats before they quit the venue, crowds of fans would never let them get away! Their presence outside a venue after a show might also put their fans' safety at risk. While 'N Sync understand the gamble they take themselves every night, they wouldn't want a fan to be hurt because of them.

Once on the bus, the guys clean up, change clothes and recover from the show. Sometimes the intensity of the emotional charge they've received from the audience leaves them speechless for quite a while. "Once we get off stage and we get on the bus, it takes us – well, it takes me a couple of hours," Chris confesses. "It's such a rush and my ears are ringing. I have to have fifteen minutes by myself just to sit and relax. To come back down and get yourself breathing at a regular pace again."

If the next stop on the tour is more than 800 miles away, 'N Sync will fly there in the morning after a good night's sleep in a hotel. If the next city on their schedule is closer, they'll all settle back for a ride of up to several hours to the next destination on their itinerary.

Fortunately, 'N Sync's tour bus is equipped for comfort. It's huge, with twelve bunks for the boys and their band, a kitchen and two common areas that function as play or meeting rooms. Both lounges have a TV, video player and stereo, so if JC and Chris want to work on a song in one area, the three remaining guys can go in the other room and play video games. Yes, 'N Sync are rich and famous, but like all boys their age, they love battling it out on a Sony PlayStation! In preparation for their third CD, 'N Sync also added a mini-recording studio to their home-from-home. It's helpful that whenever inspiration strikes – be it the middle of the afternoon or 3 a.m. in the morning – the guys of 'N Sync can always get their song ideas on tape.

Chris was the first member of 'N Sync to bring a laptop computer on the road in Europe more than two years ago. The most computer-friendly member of the group, he's got a network of fans with whom he regularly exchanges e-mails. Lately, the other guys in 'N Sync have joined the computer club. They've found all sorts of uses for their new laptops. The Internet is a great way for Justin to keep up with his family, for Lance to stay in touch with his new management company and for the rest of the guys to see what their fans are saying. Joey confessed that he sometimes uses his brother Steven's ID to chat online

anonymously with 'N Sync's fans around the world. And all the guys give their 'N Sync fan club frequent updates with the help of a little computer technology.

A while back, animal-loving Lance had an idea about taking a dog from an animal shelter on the road with the group, caring for it, and then giving it away to one lucky fan at the end of the tour. He hopes that 1999 will be the year 'N Sync finally puts his plan into action. "I was watching *Lifestyles Of The Rich And Famous*. They were talking about Adopt-A-Pet. It's where a lot of celebrities that love pets get cats and dogs adopted. We want to go to a pound and do that," he said.

Another way that the members of 'N Sync occupy themselves during a long bus ride is by going over their last show. The guys – especially JC – are quite critical of their own performance and like to reinforce the good as well as pinpoint the things that are not so good. As well as listening to the critique of their managers, like professional athletes 'N Sync's members often view a tape of their show to see themselves from the audience's perspective. "I think we're all perfectionist in what we do," observes JC. "When we're watching a dance that we do, we'll go 'Oh, we were out. We need to work on that.' We all want to be the best that we can be at what we do."

Their loyal fans expect nothing less from their five ideal guys!

> *"It's such a rush and my ears are ringing. I have to have fifteen minutes by myself just to sit and relax."*

Lance Bass
The Quiet One

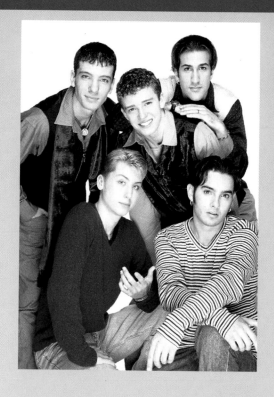

Of the five members of 'N Sync, Lance is the most surprised at the success and fame that has come his way. Yet he's always believed in the group. In fact, it was his strange premonition that 'N Sync was something special that made him get on a plane to audition in Orlando.

The weird thing is that until Lance received that fateful phone call from Justin, he had never even dared to dream of a career in music!

James Lance Bass was born in the quiet and conservative town of Laurel, Mississippi, on 4 May 1979. His family was thoroughly middle class. Father Jim is a laboratory manager while his mother Diane Bass spent many years as a middle-school math teacher. He has one older sister Stacy, now married, but still in close touch with Lance and his parents. Lance remembers Stacy's wedding to her husband Ford Lofton as one of the happiest days of his life.

Although he has something of a reputation as a laid-back guy among 'N Sync fans, his parents have said that Lance was an extremely happy and outgoing child with lots and lots of energy. Delighting in making other people laugh with jokes and pratfalls, many people suggested that Lance would one day grow up to become a comedian.

When Lance was a small child, his natural curiosity and courage got him into a bit of trouble. One time, he decided to play in the woods. He wandered into the forest near his home and lost track of time as he romped around by himself. His poor parents became so frantic that they actually called the police to help them find him. Of course, when Lance calmly showed up a few hours later, he wondered what all the fuss in front of his house was about!

Another way that little Lance occupied his time more creatively was by dressing up and putting on shows for his parents with his older sister Stacy. Lance loved to sing! As soon as he was old enough, he joined his church's choir and later, the chorus at his grammar school. In junior high school, Lance got his first taste of touring and regular live performances. He was a member of a touring choir called Attaché that travelled around the southern states of the USA competing against other choral groups.

As much as he enjoyed it, Lance didn't seriously believe he could forge a career for himself as a singer. He even doubted he would get a break as an actor, though somehow that goal seemed slightly more attainable. Still, Lance was above all a practical sort of guy. He didn't seriously believe that a kid from Clinton, Mississippi (where the family moved during Lance's grammar school years), had a chance of being "discovered." Also, Lance's parents always stressed that the way to ensure a comfortable future was by getting a good education.

Lance was a really good student. He particularly loved science and maths – two subjects that appealed to the logical and analytical part of his mind. Around middle-school age Lance dreamed of becoming an astronaut when he grew up. To that end, he spent a week in seventh grade at NASA's space camp in Cape Kennedy, Florida, with other school kids from around the country. "We had to simulate Shuttle missions and all that kind of stuff," Lance remembers. "It was incredible. After that, I was just like, that's what I want to do."

By the time he reached high school, Lance was preparing for entrance into a four-year college and still singing just for fun. His best friend Darren joined Mississippi ShowStoppers, a seven-member group that sang and danced at competitions. Lance went along because he thought it would be fun. And it was! Lance enjoyed touring around to perform at state fairs and exhibitions. Although he'd always been very athletic, ShowStoppers was the first place that Lance learned how to dance and choreograph routines.

The Low Guy

Through his participation in Mississippi ShowStoppers, Lance met Justin Timberlake's vocal coach. "See, the thing is that I didn't even have a vocal coach. I just knew the vocal coach," explained Lance about that frequent misconception. "All my friends took lessons from him and I just hung out with my friends." Regardless of how he did it, Lance made a big enough impression that when Justin called to ask for a recommendation for a fifth member of 'N Sync, the teacher handed over Lance's phone number.

Lance was sixteen and a junior in high school at the time. He had, until that point, been a very rational kid. He was Mr. Popularity at school, was on the student council and was even a member of the National Honor Society. He had two part-time jobs after school, one of which was teaching young children at a daycare center. His junior year goal was to win a scholarship to college and be awarded the class of 1997 presidency in his senior year. Clearly, Lance was not the kind of young person likely to throw away his longtime plans and follow some crazy pipe dream. Do you want more proof of his rational way of thinking? As a high-school student, the subject Lance liked best was physics! This was one extremely sensible guy!

Still, there was something about Justin's phone call that made him seriously consider flying to Orlando for the audition. "It was really weird," he said. "I never once thought, this *could* happen. It was just something that I *knew* was going to happen." Lance's parents were doubtful at first, but his mother also understood that her hard-working son had always had a secret dream of becoming a performer. How could she stand in his way? The next day, she boarded a plane bound for Orlando with her son. That afternoon found Lance singing "The Star-Spangled Banner" along with Justin, Joey, Chris and JC for the very first time. Joey always remembers that moment as one of the happiest of his life. The sound was perfect and 'N Sync had found its fifth and final member.

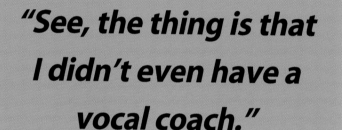

"See, the thing is that I didn't even have a vocal coach."

The first year as a member of 'N Sync was very hectic for Lance. He was working to pass his school exams through a correspondence course as well as rehearsing with the group. Although Lance's gorgeous deep voice blended with the other guys' harmonies like magic, he needed to work particularly hard on his dancing. The other four guys had much more dance experience. Lance admits that he started out as an absolutely terrible dancer! He was, however, determined to make 'N Sync work. After regular rehearsals ended, he would often stick around and rehearse dance sequences with the group's choreographer long after the others had gone home.

In addition to his new friends, Lance also had his mother Diane to turn to for some much needed encouragement and support. As he was still under the age of eighteen, his mother left her job as a teacher to be his legal guardian and to live with him in Florida. On weekends, dad Jim and Lance's older sister often made the drive down to Orlando too, so that they could all be together. For a family as close as Lance's, the separation was particularly tough.

Of course, it wasn't all hardship. Diane Bass and Justin's mother Lynn Harless got a chance to see a lot of Europe and Asia when their sons went on their first promotional tours. It was very exciting! Lance was particularly proud to be able to give his mother such a wonderful present. In 'N Sync's first year signed to BMG Munich, they spent time in Sweden, Germany, Poland, Norway, Switzerland, Holland, among other countries.

It was such a pleasant experience that touring on the road with 'N Sync has now become something of a Bass family tradition. Diane and Jim try to meet up with Lance on tour about three times a year.

Despite the geographical distance between them most of the time, the Bass family has managed to remain extremely close. Though Lance lives alone in an apartment of his own in Orlando these days, he keeps in touch with his parents and sister through daily phone calls.

Scoop!

Level-headed common sense is typical of Lance, the guy that Joey's older brother Steven nicknamed Scoop. Why the name? Well, if anyone in 'N Sync ever needs to know when they must leave for the airport or at what time they're scheduled to take a lunch break, Lance is the man to ask! He's an extremely well-organized individual who always knows what's going on! The other guys also admire Lance for his ability to think up new projects for the group – from merchandising ideas to promotional propositions to different ways to use their fan club to get closer to their audience. Lance has such a brain for business that he's even taking correspondence courses through the University of Nebraska while he's on tour with 'N Sync!

The things he's learned have already come in handy. Despite his nonstop touring and publicity schedule as a member of the group, Lance has created his own music management company called Free Lance Entertainment. He represents two clients,

country singers Meredith Edwards and Jack Defeo. How does he juggle it all? Well, most of the work that he does for his artists can be done by phone. He also gets a lot of help from his mother and sister Stacy who have joined Free Lance Entertainment as its first full-time employees.

The biggest misconception about Lance is that he's really bashful. He's not, actually. He just needs to know someone a little bit before he expresses his innermost thoughts. Like any well-raised son of the South, Lance is a complete gentleman who's polite, cheerful and nice to everyone he meets. He's also extremely friendly, a trait which, he confesses, has landed him in a load of trouble now and then.

Truthfully, Lance isn't as quiet as he used to be. Maybe all those months of sharing a room with Chris on 'N Sync's first tour rubbed off on him! These days, Lance is more ready to express his opinion during interviews, press conferences and in-store appearances. This supposed "shy guy" shocked a lot of 'N Sync's fans during the Billboard Music Awards in 1998! Kissing comedienne Kathy Griffith on stage when 'N Sync served as presenters wasn't Lance's idea – but he did enjoy all the attention that the extremely funny moment earned him!

Lance's very first girlfriend was named Bethany Dukes and he locked lips with her in front of his whole school when he was just

The biggest misconception about Lance is that he's really bashful.

five years old! The occasion was the homecoming dance at the local high school near Laurel, Mississippi. Kindergarten couple Lance and Bethany were chosen to crown the king and queen of the senior class. After delivering the crown and flowers to the reigning pair, Lance puckered up and planted a kiss on Bethany! Obviously, even as a child Lance wasn't all that shy!

Lance met his first real girlfriend, Keri Martin, at a dance in December 1991. They both arrived with their friends and connected on the dance floor where they boogied all night. It's a very happy memory for him.

This green-eyed cutie has admitted that when he wants to get a girl's attention there's nothing he won't do! He's sung under girl's windows in the moonlight and dropped a special female friend postcards from all over the world proclaiming how much he missed her. Way back in high school, he broke into the locker of the girl he fancied and arranged it so that a branch of mistletoe would spring out when she opened it. Of course, he was standing right behind her to collect his kiss when she discovered it. Such romantic gestures are not unusual for this Southern sweetheart!

Although Lance has a reputation for being pretty mellow, he does have a really great sense of fun. All of the 'N Sync guys do. They're a pack of practical jokers and, fortunately, Lance can give as good as he gets! Once, Joey played a joke on Lance by decorating his head with whipped cream and Beanie Babies (small beanbag toys) as he slept. Lance retaliated a little while later by wiping the sticky remnants of that assault all over the big guy's face and clothes! "It's all just fun," Lance said. "We're just going out and having the time of our lives."

Being the last guy to join 'N Sync wasn't the easiest situation in the world. The other boys had been friends for years when Lance joined up. At first, Chris was the one Lance knew best because the pair used to share a hotel room on tour. Later, he and Joey became closer friends by going out to nightclubs together. Justin and Lance bonded because they're the closest in age and both have a Southern background. And once Lance and JC got around to talking about books, films and music, they were friends for life. Both are very smart, very ambitious and very happy to be in 'N Sync!

While all the members of 'N Sync are athletic, Lance prefers adventurous activities to team sports. His idea of a great day is jet-skiing – preferably off of some tropical beach in Hawaii. He also loves rock climbing, hiking in the woods, in-line skating and horseback riding. Amusement parks really rate with Lance, too. He'll occasionally join in a basketball game with JC, Chris and Justin because he likes to try new things. However, he's nowhere near as good on the court as they are.

Back in Mississippi, Lance learned to ride on a horse named Toby at a summer camp sponsored by his church. When the horse died of old age a few years ago, he was extremely sad. Now that he's making money with 'N Sync, Lance dreams of owning a ranch of his own some day in the not-too-distant future. When he does, he says he'll buy a new horse and name him Toby II.

Horses aren't the only animals that Lance is crazy about. It was also his idea to bring a dog from an animal shelter on the road with the group – a plan he'd like to put in effect this year. After the tour, 'N Sync will present the dog as a gift to some deserving fan. Lance figures that not only would their puppy get a good home, but 'N Sync would also help draw attention to all the other unloved dogs and cats who need homes all around the country. Obviously, Lance cares an awful lot about animals!

Perhaps because he loves animals so much, Lance has become pretty excited about Beanie Babies, those little collectable bean bags that have been the rage in the US for a while. "I hated the idea of how stupid they were and then fans kept on giving them to us and they were like, real cute," he admitted. At last count, Lance's collection was up to more than 60 animals including special ones like the Princess Diana bear. Lance's best-loved Beanie Baby, however, is a little dog-shaped one named Toughie. Whenever Lance's parents visit him, they take home a bunch of new Beanies he's been given by fans for his collection. He's still looking for an alligator named Ally, as well as any of the extremely rare brown bear Beanies.

When it comes to music, Lance has the most wide-ranging taste of all the guys in 'N Sync. He adores R&B groups like Take 6 and Boyz II Men, but he also likes hard rockers like Offspring and more popular music from hitmakers like Matchbox 20, Celine Dion and Aerosmith. A big fan of the harmony-laden tunes of the Bee Gees, one of Lance's most exciting experiences ever was presenting the three brothers with lifetime achievement awards in Europe.

But if Lance had to name the musician he admires most, it would without a doubt be country singer Garth Brooks. At fourteen, Lance attended one of Garth's concerts and knew right then that he wanted to become a performer himself. He admires the way that Garth interacts and commands the attention of an audience. One of the songs he likes best is Garth's hit single, "The Dance." He'd love to convince his friends in 'N Sync to record their own cover version of it someday.

Like his "brothers" in 'N Sync, Lance has been thrilled that the group has taken him to so many faraway destinations. His most amazing discovery was Liechtenstein, a tiny principality only 62 square miles in area situated on the border of Switzerland and Austria. Lance has said that it is like a world out of a fairy tale, the most peaceful and beautiful place he has ever seen.

But no matter how beautiful the view is from his hotel window, homesickness follows every member of 'N Sync to every corner of the globe. How does Lance deal with it? Well, daily phone calls to his family help. He admits that the cost of his phone bill each month is astronomical!

Lance has never lost touch with his friends back home in Mississippi either. Although he didn't technically graduate with the class of 1997, he remains a part of the close-knit group of kids that he's been friendly with since grammar school. His class has held an annual reunion party each year since they graduated and Lance plans to attend 1999's festivities too. His best friends from Mississippi always know how to reach him by phone and pager. They're supportive of his career with 'N Sync, and even kind of proud. They just don't understand why girls all over the world are suddenly making a fuss over their old friend Lance!

About once a month Lance gets a chance to return home for a few days. After weeks in hotels and on tour buses and lots of late-night dinners on the run, Lance's own bed and breakfast of French toast with powdered sugar prepared by his mother are the ultimate in luxury!

Lance's Confidential File

THE FACTS

* **Name:** James Lance Bass

* **Nickname:** Lansten, Scoop, Stealth

* **Birth Date:** 4 May 1979

* **Birthplace:** Laurel, Mississippi

* **Hometown:** Clinton, Mississippi

* **Height and Weight:** 5ft 10in tall, 155lb

* **Hair and Eyes:** Blond and green

* **Parents:** Jim and Diane Bass

* **Sister:** Married sister Stacy Lofton

* **Religion:** Baptist

* **Car:** Toyota 4-runner in black

* **Shoe Size:** 11

* **First Kiss:** Bethany, aged five

* **Unique Collections:** Beanie Babies and Taz dolls

* **Super Secret:** Lance has a tiny tattoo of flames on his right ankle!

LANCE'S LOVES

✶ **Music:** Garth Brooks, Celine Dion, Matchbox 20, Aerosmith

✶ **Actors:** Tom Hanks, Nicholas Cage, Rosie O'Donnell, Helen Hunt, Meg Ryan

✶ **Films:** *Armageddon, Clue*

✶ **TV Shows:** *I Love Lucy* and *Third Rock From The Sun*

✶ *South Park* **Characters:** Cartman and Stan

✶ **Celebrity Crush:** Country singer Shania Twain

✶ **Video Game:** *Bug*

✶ **Non-'N Sync Song:** "The Dance"

✶ **Food:** Mexican

✶ **Breakfast Treat:** French toast topped with powdered sugar

✶ **Hot Drink:** Almond cappuccino

✶ **Sports:** Jet-skiing, baseball, volleyball

✶ **Place To Visit:** Liechtenstein

✶ **Gift From A Fan:** Hard-to-find Beanie Baby

✶ **Lance's Advice:** "Just live it up. Live every day like it's your last."

'N Sync In Love!

'N Sync fans are some of the most vocal and enthusiastic on the planet. They love the group's songs, respect their talent and believe that Chris, JC, Justin, Joey and Lance are five of the most gorgeous guys to ever grace the pop charts.

Fortunately for their fans, the boys of 'N Sync are also five of the most eligible single guys around! Justin, Joey, Lance, Chris and JC all confess that they do date when they have a chance; however, they just don't have the free time to pursue a long-lasting relationship right now. Would any of the members of 'N Sync date one of their fans? Sure! Whether a girl likes or dislikes 'N Sync's tunes isn't as important to the guys as finding someone that they can have fun with.

Justin: The Talkative One

While Justin can certainly appreciate a drop-dead gorgeous girl, he looks for more than a pretty face when it comes to spending time with someone. After all, he reasons, if he can't talk to or have fun with someone, what's the point of being with her?

Justin likes girls who are optimistic and tend to look on the bright side of life. Chronic complainers need not apply! In this world of "sarcasm and pessimism," he's said, a sunny smile and a positive outlook are extremely hard to find. But he still has hopes of finding his cheerful other half. After all, Justin is basically a happy guy, why would he want to hang around someone who brings him down?

Justin likes girls who are self-confident. Self-assured girls are much more fun to be around because they don't need constant approval from him. They already know and like themselves. Mind you, these are not girls who shout from the rooftops about how great they are, because Justin can't tolerate conceited people, but rather girls who possess an inner strength just to be who they are. They're completely honest, a quality that's very important to Justin.

On the other hand, girls who are emotionally needy make Justin want to run and hide! "Do I look good?" "Am I the prettiest girl in the room?" "Do you really like me?" Plaguing Justin with questions full of self-doubt is a real turn-off!

Similarly, clingy girls who never leave his side make Justin feel suffocated. He likes to circulate and meet new people at a party and he expects his date to do the same. Not a particularly jealous guy himself, Justin has little patience for possessive girls.

Girls who leap to quick judgements about others also turn off Justin. In his travels around the world, he's met a lot of people and this experience has really opened up his view. He can't help but think that people who are intolerant or who prejudge others are simply ignorant. He doesn't have time for girls like that. This chatty guy talks an awful lot, so he'd love to find a girl who's a good listener. Of course, he'd also enjoy a date mate who isn't shy about voicing her opinion too!

Sitting around and moaning about the fate of the world is simply not Justin's style. He loves to laugh. A funny guy himself, Justin really appreciates people who can make him laugh, so girls who can make him chuckle are especially awesome! He also appreciates someone who is spontaneous, youthful and fun. He's always up for a new adventure and he treasures the company of friends who are too.

Although Justin calls himself a romantic, he thinks some of the traditional "romantic dates," like fancy dinners, are overrated! He's not into boring nights. For Justin, a fabulous date might be something more daring – like climbing to the top of a hill together to get a bird's eye view of the city lights below. He also likes nightlife, so dancing the night away at a party or club with someone special is a fun alternative too.

Justin likes girls who are optimistic and tend to look on the bright side of life.

Adventurous girls who love the outdoors really rate with Justin. Trapped inside hotel rooms, planes and tour buses for so much of the time, he's come to relish his rare hours outdoors. Someone who could keep up with him physically as he hikes the woods and climbs rocks would be a prized partner. Justin would love to find a really daring girl willing to go bungee jumping with him! Finally, he would love to meet a girl who appreciates basketball and could cheer along with him and support his basketball team on a winter's afternoon!

It's easy to discover a little more personal information on Justin by looking at his Zodiac sign. An Aquarian, born on 31 January 1981, Justin is an extremely social person who communicates easily with others. He can be extremely chatty, so he enjoys speaking to people who are good listeners and who aren't shy about contributing to a conversation.

He's a really nice guy! That's because people like Justin, who are born under the sign of the Water Bearer, are motivated by kindness. They love being liked, so they will do anything in their power to make others happy. Often considered the "humanitarians" of the Zodiac, Justin and his Aquarian brothers and sisters are very sympathetic to the needs and desires of their friends. They're loyal, compassionate, and smart too.

It's no surprise that Justin has adjusted so well to his hectic life on the road with 'N Sync, because as an Aquarian, he's extremely adaptable. He has a positive outlook, a healthy love of life and adjusts well to almost any situation that comes his way. New people, new situations, new places – Justin greets them all with a

smile and an eagerness to discover something different. He craves new experiences and adventures!

In matters of the heart, Justin's Zodiac sign suggests that he might find his perfect match with a girl born under the signs of Gemini, Libra, Aries or Sagittarius.

Gemini girls possess the intelligence and quick-wittedness that Justin most appreciates. Both clever and inventive, they're always up for a new challenge! Like Justin, they're happy to try new things and are very adaptable.

Ladies born under the sign of Libra are often serene and beautiful – both inside and out. They have the unique ability to charm Justin out of any bad moods. They're also extremely tolerant – an important quality to look for in a romantic mate if you happen to be a pop star spending more than half the year on the road!

Girls born under the sign of Aries have an enthusiasm for life that attracts upbeat guys like Justin like moths to a flame. They're energetic, spontaneous and fun – all characteristics Justin enjoys in a girlfriend.

Finally, independent Sagittarian girls present an irresistible challenge to an

Aquarian like Justin. These outgoing and bubbly people possess an inner spark that lights up a room as they enter. They like being the focus of attention and enjoy life to the fullest. Paired up with another attention-getter like Justin, they would form a unique and admired couple.

JC: The Classic Romantic

It's no great surprise that confident girls really rate with JC too! He and Justin are such good friends that it's only natural that they'd share similar tastes in girls. But while Justin is drawn to extremely outgoing girls, JC prefers young ladies who express their confidence in a more understated fashion.

JC's the kind of romantic guy who believes in love at first sight. His fantasy is to lock eyes with the girl of his dreams across the crowded floor of a party and then proceed to sweep her off her feet. JC notices a girl's eyes first. He has said that he'd never be comfortable with a girl who couldn't look him in the eye because trust is very necessary to him in a relationship. He admires someone who is secure enough in herself really to enjoy life. People who spend all their time fretting about their appearance just can't let go and have fun, he reasons.

A workaholic like JC definitely needs someone who will force him to slow down and take a day off once in a while. A girl who can make a gentle but convincing argument about why he should put down his guitar and come to the party would be greatly appreciated! JC also enjoys going out in-line skating, dancing, hiking and more; it's just that he often needs to be reminded to pursue these hobbies more frequently.

JC could only have a lasting relationship with a girl who is patient. His ambition and his schedule don't give him a lot of free time, so it's important that a potential love match should realize that he's not going to be around as much as a "normal" boyfriend. JC really appreciates girls who are nurturing, supportive and sympathetic. If his girl has plans and dreams of her own to keep her occupied during his long absences, he would feel happier still!

If someone is willing to put up with JC's hectic schedule, the time she does spend with him will be worth the wait. Although JC claims that he's "boring" when it comes to romance, he just means he's more traditional than the other guys in the group are. He likes giving girls flowers and taking them out to see a romantic comedy at the cinema. A candle-lit dinner followed by a play (but not a musical!) is JC's idea of a perfect romantic night out. Somewhat of a homebody, JC also thinks that cuddling up in front of the TV with someone special, a bowl of popcorn and a good film in the video player is a perfect night in!

A girl who appreciates the literary classics would be a good match for JC. That's because he would love to find a special someone to accompany him to his choice of event of the year, Orlando's Shakespeare festival. Each spring, one of the Bard's famous plays is performed outdoors by the edge of a lake. For JC, it's the perfect combination of fun and romance!

Born under the sign of Leo the Lion on 8 August 1976, JC possesses a fierce determination to create, innovate and lead the way. It's no wonder so many Leos become performers because they absolutely thrive when they are the focus of attention. People born under this self-assured sign are terrific leaders who draw others to themselves effortlessly. Leos like JC have a lot of energy and ideas about how to change the world. Their mega-confidence is so strong that it can actually rub off on their friends, making them feel more alive and self-assured too!

With so much fire in their personality, it's important that Leos like JC pair up with partners who are able to restrain their ambitions from burning wildly out of control. Leos' self-confidence must be

Leos like JC have a lot of energy and ideas about how to change the world.

tempered with humility so that they remain lovable instead of demanding and conceited. That's where supportive friends, family members and romantic partners are needed.

Leos like JC might find their best love matches with girls born under the signs of Aries, Sagittarius, Gemini, and Libra.

Girls born under the sign of Aries are optimistic and energetic. Their view of the world as a place where dreams come true definitely meshes with JC's optimistic beliefs. He also respects all Aries' courage to express exactly what she thinks to anyone. Again, JC cherishes honesty in his relationships.

Good-natured Sagittarian girls have personalities that positively sparkle! Even a single-minded guy like JC is coaxed to put his work down and join in by her contagious laughter. She's

precisely the kind of girl who'll know how to soothe her Leo's worries away and persuade him to have a little fun!

A Gemini girl is a good match for a Leo like JC because she stimulates his mind with her confident and thoughtful personality. She can go with the flow totally and enjoys spontaneous words of romance. She's as good at creating a romantic moment herself as she is appreciative of her guy's unexpected sentimental gesture.

A Libran girl is charming in almost any situation and appreciates the nice things others do for her. She's fun and romantic – qualities an old fashioned boy like JC definitely appreciates. Her calm, well-balanced approach to life really makes him miss her when he's away.

Lance: The Southern Gentleman

In early 1999, Lance was unsettled by gossip linking him romantically with Danielle Fishel, the eighteen-year-old actress who plays Topanga on the popular US TV teen comedy *Boy Meets World*. Though the pair do not deny being friends – Danielle was photographed hanging out backstage with 'N Sync at the Billboard Music Awards – Lance has said that they've only seen each other a few times since meeting in November 1998. That hardly counts as the romance of the century!

Adorable green-eyed Lance says that he's never been in love. Though it's an experience he looks forward to enjoying, he's willing to wait. His commitment to 'N Sync as well as his outside business ventures make it completely impossible for Lance to invest time in a steady relationship right now. Someday when he does give away his heart, he wants to be able to give that extremely lucky girl his undivided attention. He's the kind of guy who expects love to last forever.

What kind of girl makes Lance sit up and notice? Well, like JC, he thinks a girl's eyes are her most attractive feature. Some say that eyes are the windows to the soul, and Lance would probably agree. The qualities that he looks for in a potential date are things a person can reveal through her eyes like honesty, innocence, good morals and a super sense of fun. "My ideal girl is not someone that I'm physically attracted to at first," he said. "We just totally hit it off as best friends for a while and then it grows into something."

Although he's left his small hometown behind, Lance still respects the morals and values he was brought up with. His faith is so important to him that he carries an inspirational book called *What Would Jesus Do?* with him on tour. Finding a mate who shares his beliefs is very important to Lance, who admits that he likes "good girls" who are innocent, sweet and willing to open up and become his closest friend in the world.

However, just because a girl is nice doesn't mean she can't be fun too! Lance and his 'N Sync brothers joke around a lot, so he appreciates a girl who can laugh at herself. Someone who's super serious or moody wouldn't last long among the 'N Sync gang. Lance and the rest of the boys like to tease and play silly pranks to relieve some of the tension and a girl needs to be confident enough not to take such things personally. It's a wise girl who arms herself with her own clever ripostes when she hangs around with these boys!

Strength of the physical variety is a major plus around Lance too. This self-confessed beach bum isn't content to laze away an afternoon just lying on a blanket. He'd rather spend a summer afternoon jet-skiing, water-skiing or parasailing! It takes a healthy and energetic girl to keep up with Lance's idea of a great date.

If he's forced to remain on dry land, count on Lance to find something adventurous to do. He thinks heights are thrilling, so rock climbing and hiking up mountains is his idea of a fun time. He's never explored a cave before, but he thinks it would be really cool to try. Another great date would be a trip to an amusement park to ride the rollercoasters that Lance loves so much.

This Southern boy also enjoys horseback riding – he's been doing it since he was a little kid. In fact, as a child he thought he'd like to become a rodeo rider but he could never land his tricks just right. So when riding with Lance, it's best to be prepared for something more strenuous than a sedate trot across a meadow!

Lance's birthday on 4 May 1979 puts him firmly under the sign of Taurus, the Bull. While people born under this Sun sign are notoriously stubborn, that doesn't have to be a bad thing. In matters of the heart, Taureans like Lance are deeply loyal and crave stability. Once his mind is made up, you can be sure he won't flirt around or cheat.

Taurean guys like Lance are willing to wait for the right girl too. They're extraordinarily patient in all things, but especially love. Girls born under the signs of Capricorn, Virgo, Pisces and Cancer are Lance's best horoscope matches.

Lance and his Taurean brothers appreciate the steadiness of a Capricorn girl. She alone of all the other signs is just as reliable and stable as a Taurean. She's also very motivated to pursue a career of her own and smart enough to do well – two qualities with which Taurus can definitely identify.

Earthy girls born under the sign of Virgo appeal to Taureans because so many of them enjoy and respect the great outdoors too. Loyal and comforting to be around, a Virgo girl offers a dose of reality in a crazy mixed-up world. This honest girl will always let him know the real score!

Dreamy Piscean girls have a creative streak that a guy like Lance can really admire. Many girls born under this sign are musical or active in the arts in some way. These romantics are sweet and kind to others – qualities that Lance certainly respects in anyone!

Finally, girls born under the sign of Cancer exhibit affection and ambition in equal parts. When paired with a Taurean like Lance, they create a strong couple who would be supportive and nurturing of one another's goals and ideals. Together, both partners give each other the strength and willpower to succeed.

Lance is the kind of guy who expects love to last forever.

Chris: The Seeker

Crazy, outgoing Chris has a sensitive side that is always in search of a soulmate. He has a good idea of what she'll be like too: a girl with a great smile and pretty eyes, who is friendly, enthusiastic and willing to act a little silly. She doesn't spend a lot of time worrying about what others think of her. She loves the beach, sunny days, music and little kids. It would also help if Chris' dream girl likes rollercoasters, rap music, dancing, in-line skating and tolerates unusual hairstyles. He thinks that a girl who's confident enough to make the first move is a real turn-on too!

Chris also has a very clear idea about what qualities his perfect mate wouldn't have! A girl who is controlling, greedy or obsessive is not the girl for him.

With so much of his life planned by 'N Sync's managers, Chris likes to be very impulsive during his free time. Someone who's also willing to let the moment determine the action is really appealing to Chris. And, of course, this wise guy hopes to find someone who will laugh at most of his jokes!

Chris thinks that an afternoon on a secluded beach would be the ideal romantic date. Perhaps a swim or a little surfboarding would start the day, followed by a picnic lunch. That evening, he'd take his perfect date out for a night of great live music and dancing.

Chris is a Libran, born on 17 October 1971. Like the scales that symbolize this sign, he's a very fair-minded guy who's impartial and always ready to listen to reason. He has a great need to share – his feelings, his good fortune and his opinions are all up for grabs by any sympathetic soul who catches his imagination. A natural cheerleader, he's great at encouraging others to reach for the skies. His support is an inspiration to most of the people in his life.

> ## *Chris thinks that a girl who's confident enough to make the first move is a real turn-on too!*

According to the Zodiac, Chris' best match would occur with a girl born under the signs of Gemini, Aquarius, Leo or Sagittarius. Gemini girls can be friendly and free-spirited; two qualities that are likely to appeal to an extrovert Libran like Chris. He would also find her commitment to her community in tune with his own dedication to making the world a better place.

Likewise, the open-minded Aquarian girl is a big turn-on for the balanced Libran boy. She's just as impatient with injustice and intolerance as he is – plus, she's willing to do something about it. Girls born under the sign of Aquarius are often very talkative and intelligent. When paired with an equally expressive and bright Libran like Chris, she can expect lots of deep, intellectually stimulating conversations.

Leo girls are attractive for the energy and enthusiasm they bring to any activity they undertake. Like Libran boys, they also enjoy being the focus of attention. They're charming, stylish, fun and have a flair for the dramatic that an expressive guy like Chris could really appreciate. Like Librans, many Leos are also drawn to music and the arts, making it easy to form the perfect collaboration with a talented guy like Chris.

Libran boys prize Sagittarian girls for their natural intelligence and insight. Like Chris and his fellow Libran brothers, these girls have a very strong sense of fair play that would never allow them to take advantage of another. Sincere and honest, Sagittarian girls make a good match for the similarly principled Libran boy.

Joey: The Tease

Don't believe that Joey is insincere because he's such a ladies man, he'd be willing to trade in his licence to flirt if only the right girl would come along! This good-hearted guy is attracted to a girl with a brilliant smile. He thinks girls who are honest, affectionate, well-groomed and outgoing are particularly enticing.

Growing up in a large, expressive family encouraged Joey to talk about the things on his mind. He doesn't think there's any problem that can't be helped by talking about it. A social girl who isn't afraid to express her opinions would be a perfect match for him. A girl needs to know that she should "just be herself" if she's going to hang around with this affectionate guy.

The most romantic thing that Joey has ever done for a girl is send her flowers – lots and lots of flowers. The occasion was his ex-girlfriend's birthday. Joey, in the ultimate romantic gesture, arranged to send her flowers once every hour while she was at work.

For Joey, the perfect date would be a night on the town.

For Joey, the perfect date would be a night on the town. He's a big film fan who enjoys everything from action/adventure to serious drama. Most of his free nights start with a date at the cinema. On most evenings, Joey's also up for going clubbing afterwards, so if a girl loves to dance she's in for a great time. His choice of clubs are those that play techno or top 40 music – including maybe an 'N Sync song or two!

Born on 28 January 1977, Joey's Zodiac sign – like Justin's – is Aquarius, the Water Bearer. Blessed with a mild-temperament, Joey is one of the Zodiac's major "people persons." He just can't help but be curious about the people whom he meets and his effortless social skills give him the tools to draw them out. Few people can resist the charming attentions of an Aquarian boy like Joey!

Always excited by new experiences, an Aquarian like Joey greets each day as the beginning of a new adventure. When it comes to a long-term partner, he seeks a girl who shares the same enthusiasm for living. Girls born under the signs of Gemini, Libra, Aries and Sagittarius are particularly well equipped for the job!

Gemini girls are resourceful – they can crack a joke, fix a puncture and cook a meal all in the same evening. Aquarians like Joey are fascinated by their ability to rise to any challenge.

Aquarian boys turn to Libran girls for a breath of fresh air. Their reassuring personalities make simply anything seem possible. These girls rarely have self-doubts and they make their lucky partners feel more confident too.

Arian girls practically crackle with energy and enthusiasm. They have lots of original ideas and dreams that provide fuel for a creative Aquarian guy like Joey.

Finally, the outgoing Sagittarian girl attracts Joey and his Aquarian brothers with her magnetic animation. She commands attention just by being her feisty and confident self. An Aquarian guy like Joey can't help but notice!

Chris Kirkpatrick
The Funny One

Although all the members of 'N Sync are better than most at making people laugh, there's no question that the guy with the funniest wisecracks is Chris Kirkpatrick. Able to arouse a smile with a glance, provoke helpless giggles with a word and create outright hysteria with a joke, Chris wins the funniest 'N Sync member award hands down!

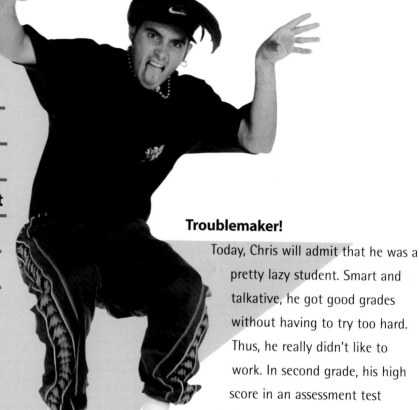

For much of his life, Chris has used laughter as an antidote to life's troubles. Over the years, it's helped him make friends, win over playground bullies, and forget the things that have caused him pain in his young life.

Born on 17 October 1971 in Clarion, Pennsylvania, a town about 60 miles northeast of Pittsburgh, Christopher Alan Kirkpatrick was raised in a single-parent household by his mother, Beverly Eustice. In those early years, they didn't have a lot of money and they moved around a lot. Chris and his expanding family – half-sisters Molly, Kate, Emily and Taylor range in age from 24 to six – lived in the states of Pennsylvania, Ohio and California while he was growing up. Being the funniest kid in class was a way for Chris to earn acceptance whenever he found himself faced with being the "new kid" at school again.

Troublemaker!

Today, Chris will admit that he was a pretty lazy student. Smart and talkative, he got good grades without having to try too hard. Thus, he really didn't like to work. In second grade, his high score in an assessment test indicated that he belonged in a more accelerated class for "gifted" children. Instead of it being a worthwhile experience, his separation from his friends was the cause of Chris' feelings of alienation. "I was a troublemaker," he confesses today. "I totally hated being there. I just didn't have anything in common with [the other kids in the class]." Although he was just as smart as the other students, Chris acted the clown, getting in trouble for mouthing off in class and running around getting dirty during break.

The ability to sing and play music was as common a trait in Chris' family as blue eyes are in other families.

The one thing that remained constant in Chris's life was music. His mother Beverly is a voice teacher. His grandparents sang professionally, too – his grandfather released five albums as a country-and-western performer and Chris's grandmother was a trained opera singer. Cousins, aunts, uncles – everyone on his mother's side of the family sang. The ability to sing and play music was as common a trait in Chris's family as blue eyes are in other families. Nobody thought much about it, because all their relations shared the same talent!

Chris started singing as a child in church musicals which his mother often directed. He also was a member of his school's choir. But it wasn't until he auditioned for a role in a school production of the musical *Oliver* that Chris realized he wanted a career in entertainment. Encouraged to audition for the show by his school choir director, Chris had expected to get a part in the chorus or maybe be chosen to play one of the gang of young pickpockets in the cast. He was shocked to learn that he'd actually landed the role of the lead character, Oliver Twist. Best of all, Chris, the undisciplined school troublemaker, really rose to the occasion. He devoted all his time to rehearsals and had a wonderful time during the run of the show. Taking his bow and getting the biggest round of applause made him realize right then that he wanted to become a professional performer. It made him so happy.

For the rest of his high school career, Chris took every opportunity to appear on stage. He played American football (to enjoy a different sort of limelight) and was president of his school's choir.

After graduating from high school, Chris moved in with his father, Byron Kirkpatrick, in Orlando, Florida, to take advantage of the entertainment scene that was thriving there in 1990. With so many studios and theme parks hiring entertainers, there was a lot of work in the Sunshine State for young people. Thinking he would become an actor, Chris enrolled in Valencia College and began taking courses in the dramatic arts. During his second term, he also began singing in the school's chorus.

By an odd stroke of irony, future Backstreet Boy Howie Dorough was also a member of the choir at Valencia College. If Chris and Howie had been friends back then, Chris might have ended up in that *other* Orlando vocal group and 'N Sync might not have been created! Chris and Howie, however, were complete opposites in personality in those days – Howie was quiet and serious while Chris, of course, was loud and boisterous.

So, when Howie started asking a few of his fellow choir members to audition for his new group, Chris wasn't invited. But Chris's best friend was! Although he would eventually leave Backstreet Boys himself, his friend stuck around long enough to introduce Chris to the Backstreet Boys' business manager, Louis Pearlman. A little while later, Big Papa (as his Trans Continental recording artists call him) would become instrumental in the success of 'N Sync.

But Chris had a lot to learn first. His gorgeous voice – he had discovered his awesome high falsetto and baritone-tenor voice by this time – won him a scholarship to Rollins College, a prestigious school also in the Orlando area. Taking courses in both music and psychology, Chris briefly toyed with the idea of becoming a psychologist. It wasn't as odd a choice as it sounds, because

sensitive Chris really is a people person. He thought, perhaps, that music therapy – reaching troubled patients through the use of music – might be a natural outgrowth of the things he loved best.

Yet in the end, music ended up winning Chris's true devotion. He needed to sing and perform for others. Chris was also fortunate enough to come under the influence of a very special music teacher who helped him focus his energies on his future. "I've been a punk all my life...but this guy, Dr. Sinclair, was the first choir director that I ever had that was willing to take a chance on me," said Chris. Noticing not only Chris's talent, but also the good heart he so skillfully hid under a wisecracking exterior, the teacher took him under his wing. He advised Chris on what courses to pursue, how to apply for scholarship money and how to hone his natural gifts as a performer. Years later, when Chris received his first gold record with 'N Sync, he gave one to his former mentor. A man, Chris has said, that will always remain an inspiration to him.

> ## "I've been a punk all my life...but this guy, Dr. Sinclair, was the first choir director that I ever had that was willing to take a chance on me,"

Though his voice won him some money for college, Chris also took a lot of odd jobs to pay for his living expenses. For a while, he sang R.E.M. and Pearl Jam songs with his friends at coffee shops for money. He formed a vocal harmony group. He even provided some Christmas spirit by singing with the Caroling Company. Through this seasonal job – singing Christmas carols at the theme parks and other tourist destinations during the holiday season – Chris hooked up with the Hollywood Hightones, a doo-wop group who performed a regular gig at Universal Studios Theme Park. For more than three years, Chris, two other guys and a girl, sang *a cappella* versions of old 1950s chestnuts like "Rock Around the Clock" and "The Lion Sleeps Tonight" six times a day. Entertaining the tourists was great preparation for Chris's eventual job as a bona fide pop star!

It was 1995 when a 24-year-old Chris realized that if he really wanted to succeed in the music industry he needed to form his own group. Finding partners who were also ready to make a complete all-or-nothing commitment was the hard part. First, he recruited Joey Fatone, a dynamic singer and dancer who also worked at Universal Studios. He also invited Justin Timberlake, a talented former member of the *Mickey Mouse Club* whom he'd met on the Orlando audition circuit. In turn, Justin brought in JC Chasez, another *MMC* kid. Eventually, the group added Lance Bass as their fifth member.

In Private

Even when he's away from the spotlight, Chris has a clever quip for every occasion. That's one of the reasons little children love him. He especially good with his youngest sister Taylor and his three little nephews. Whenever he's home on a break, "Uncle Chris" becomes all the kids' best playmate. That's because, even though he's the oldest member of the group, he's actually the biggest kid of them all!

This generosity of spirit extends to his reactions to his fans and the people that he meets off stage. When a little girl in his apartment complex discovered that one of her heroes lived right upstairs, he was nice enough to give her an autographed CD. Although he asked her not to tell all her friends where he lived, he really doesn't mind the attention! After all, his distinctive braids make Chris stand out in a crowd no matter where he goes!

The eldest member of 'N Sync has had several serious girlfriends, but like his friends in the group, he's very single these

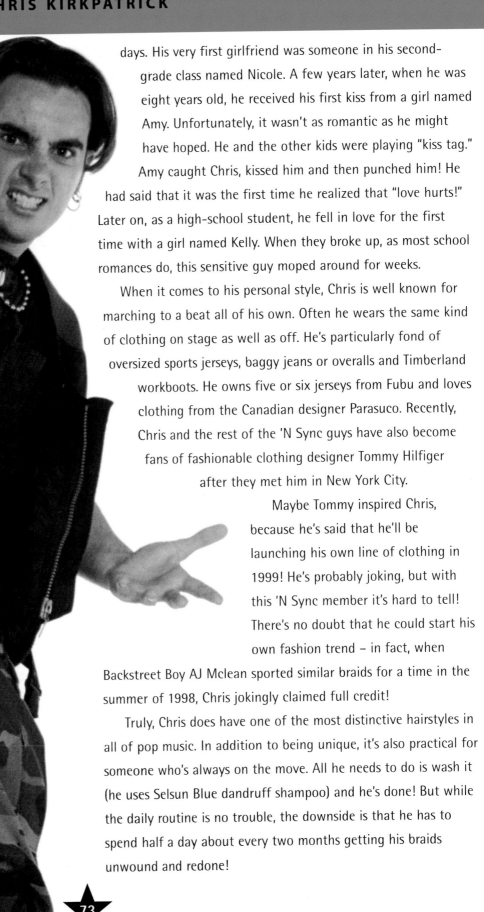

days. His very first girlfriend was someone in his second-grade class named Nicole. A few years later, when he was eight years old, he received his first kiss from a girl named Amy. Unfortunately, it wasn't as romantic as he might have hoped. He and the other kids were playing "kiss tag." Amy caught Chris, kissed him and then punched him! He had said that it was the first time he realized that "love hurts!" Later on, as a high-school student, he fell in love for the first time with a girl named Kelly. When they broke up, as most school romances do, this sensitive guy moped around for weeks.

When it comes to his personal style, Chris is well known for marching to a beat all of his own. Often he wears the same kind of clothing on stage as well as off. He's particularly fond of oversized sports jerseys, baggy jeans or overalls and Timberland workboots. He owns five or six jerseys from Fubu and loves clothing from the Canadian designer Parasuco. Recently, Chris and the rest of the 'N Sync guys have also become fans of fashionable clothing designer Tommy Hilfiger after they met him in New York City.

Maybe Tommy inspired Chris, because he's said that he'll be launching his own line of clothing in 1999! He's probably joking, but with this 'N Sync member it's hard to tell! There's no doubt that he could start his own fashion trend – in fact, when Backstreet Boy AJ Mclean sported similar braids for a time in the summer of 1998, Chris jokingly claimed full credit!

Truly, Chris does have one of the most distinctive hairstyles in all of pop music. In addition to being unique, it's also practical for someone who's always on the move. All he needs to do is wash it (he uses Selsun Blue dandruff shampoo) and he's done! But while the daily routine is no trouble, the downside is that he has to spend half a day about every two months getting his braids unwound and redone!

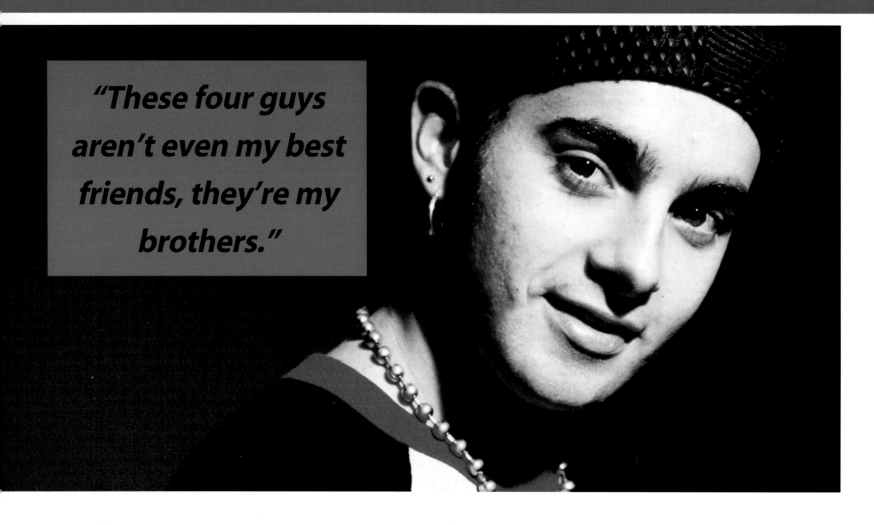

"These four guys aren't even my best friends, they're my brothers."

When Chris has some spare time, he likes to perform martial arts and he enjoys skateboarding around town. Despite his success as a singer, he still doesn't own a car! Chris says he'd rather walk, bike or skateboard so he can actually see some of where he's going. He claims his perfect day would be skating to the beach for surfing and a picnic with a female friend, followed by a night of partying. Chris would like to top it off with a good few hours' rest and then do it all again!

Or a day out at a gridiron football game would be good. Sports have always been a huge part of Chris's life. He can debate the injustice of the 1998-1999 professional basketball players' strike or the reasons for his tips in this year's Superbowl for hours. While he shoots a lot of basketball hoops with Justin and JC on tour, his preferred sport is American football.

Being a small kid compared to his classmates never stopped Chris from risking life and limb on muddy football fields as a child. Chris brags that his most beloved toy was a little American fooball he used to like to chew on as an infant! He played football in both junior and senior high school and he absolutely loved it. Today, he still roots for his home state teams. He's a devoted follower of the Pittsburgh Steelers in the professional arena, and the Penn State Nittany Lions at the college level.

When Chris moved to Florida as a college student, he discovered the joy of surfing. He tries to soak up as much sun and beach life as possible when he's home. He's also looking forward to a future 'N Sync tour that might take him to some of the world's greatest surfing spots like Hawaii and Australia. He just hasn't figured out a way to cart his surfboard along yet!

Chris admits that he's taken some dangerous chances on his surfboard – like the time he surfed the enormous waves churned up by a hurricane off the coast of Florida!

Chris likes to live dangerously on land too. On tour, he's 'N Sync's party animal who always has enough energy to go out clubbing after a show. He loves to explore the nightlife in a new city. He doesn't even care what type of music is playing, just as long as there's dancing. Chris also enjoys going to other people's concerts – some performers he loves to see live are Boyz II Men, Busta Rhymes, Missy Elliot and the Beastie Boys. At a hot show, Chris can forget all about his responsibilities to 'N Sync and just lose himself in the music like every other fan!

And speaking of fans, Chris is absolutely amazing about keeping in touch with 'N Sync's friends online. Although the other guys in 'N Sync have finally bought laptop computers of their own, Chris has had his for years. He regularly exchanges e-mail with 'N Sync fans from all over the world. In fact, some days he will download as many as 300 letters from his fans. He also enjoys surfing the World Wide Web to see what people are saying about 'N Sync. For Chris, constructive criticism is a great way to find out where there's room for improvement.

Chris feels really excited about the possibility of improving 'N Sync's future recordings. He's proud of the group's debut and Christmas albums, but he knows there's much more to learn in the recording studio. Up until now, the 'N Sync song he likes best is "Giddy Up" because the entire group had a hand in writing it. For the new CD, he has worked with Justin to create new raps and sat down with JC to figure out the lyrics of a new love song. His overall goal is for 'N Sync's music to retain its party feel while growing along with the taste of their fans and the overall evolution of pop music.

Obviously, as the founding father of 'N Sync, Chris is justifiably proud of all that the group has accomplished in such a short time. While 'N Sync's gold and platinum records certainly bring a smile to his face, one of the things that has given him the greatest satisfaction is the tight bond he's achieved with the other guys in the group. "These four guys aren't even my best friends, they're my brothers," he's said. "I think the closeness has always been there since we were friends before and since we're still friends. You get closer as you go on. Doing interview after interview, people are answering questions. Now, there's really nothing about the other guys that I don't know."

As much as Chris enjoys the attention he receives from fans, he gets a bigger charge out of watching girls scream for Justin or seeing audience members surround Lance hoping for an autograph. He enjoys succeeding himself, but he loves sitting back and watching the other guys in the group triumph! After so much time spent with so many groups that didn't work out, Chris is delighted to have such terrific "brothers" with whom to share the biggest adventure of his life.

Chris's Confidential File

THE FACTS

* **Name:** Christopher Alan Kirkpatrick

* **Nicknames:** Psycho, Crazy, Lucky, Puerto Rico

* **Birth Date:** 17 October 1971

* **Birthplace:** Clarion, Pennsylvania

* **Height and Weight:** 5ft 9in tall, 155lb

* **Hair and Eyes:** Brown and brown

* **Mother:** Beverly Eustice

* **Sisters:** Molly, Kate, Emily and Taylor

* **Religion:** Lutheran

* **Shoe Size:** 7½

* **First Kiss:** Amy, aged eight

* **Unique Collection:** Records! The vinyl kind.

* **Super Secret:** Chris sometimes wears glasses

CHRIS'S LOVES

⭐ **Music:** Busta Rhymes, Brian McKnight, Dru Hill, Boyz II Men

⭐ **Actors:** Adam Sandler, Jackie Chan, Bruce Lee, Mel Gibson

⭐ **Films:** *The Waterboy, Happy Gilmore, Star Wars*

⭐ **TV Show:** *South Park*

⭐ ***South Park* Character:** Eric Cartman

⭐ **Comic Book Character:** Spiderman

⭐ **Celebrity Crush:** Gwen Stefani of No Doubt

⭐ **Video Game:** *Final Fantasy 7* on PlayStation

⭐ **Food:** Tacos

⭐ **Cereal:** Cap `N Crunch with Crunchberries

⭐ **Candy:** M&M's, especially the green ones!

⭐ **Hot Drink:** Tea

⭐ **Sport:** American football

⭐ **Professional Sports Team:** Pittsburgh Steelers

⭐ **College Teams:** Penn State and Ohio State

⭐ **Theme Park Ride:** Koomba at Busch Gardens in Tampa, Florida

⭐ **Place To Visit:** California

⭐ **Gift From A Fan:** Two original Bruce Lee autographs

⭐ **Chris' Advice:** "Just be yourself."

Joey Fatone
The Flirty One

Joey Fatone's portable phone gets the hardest workout because he's always chatting with someone! Good natured, positive, talkative and flirtatious, Joey just can't help himself. He's always been everyone's pal and, since joining 'N Sync, he's made friends all over the world!

Baby Joseph Anthony Fatone, Jr. was born on 28 January 1977 at Victory Memorial Hospital in Brooklyn, New York. Although there's not documented proof, it's almost certain that he came into the world with a smile! The youngest child of Joseph Sr. and Phyllis – he's got two older siblings, Janine who's 26 and 24-year-old Steven – was a good kid, but extremely hyperactive and excitable.

Around the age of eight, he secured a towel around his shoulders with a safety pin and attempted to fly out of a window like his hero, Superman. Thank goodness he was only on the second floor and he'd had the forethought to put a thin mattress under his window just in case! Still, adventures like that brought Joey and his parents to the hospital emergency room so many times that the doctors and nurses on call got to know his name! It wasn't the bruises and cuts they treated that were so memorable, instead it was the little boy's bright smile and funny

charm that won them over! "I was the kid that everyone knew and everyone got along with," Joey remembers.

Like most kids in the district he called home, Joey attended a private Catholic school named St. Mary's where he was required to wear the standard uniform of a white shirt, dark trousers and a tie. Although he liked his school, it didn't provide many extracurricular activities for a kid as lively as Joey. Fortunately, his father realized that this was what the community lacked and decided to do something about it.

Joseph Fatone, Sr., who today works for a telephone company, sang professionally for many years with a locally famous vocal group called The Orions (pronounced *or-EE-ons*) and ran his own local drama troupe. Around the Christmas holidays each year, he would help put on a play as a benefit to raise money for the church. Starting when he was five, Joey was always an eager participant in these community plays. His brother and sister would always be part of the show too. Acting and music were very popular pastimes in the Fatone household.

Joey discovered his love of singing very early in life. His dad's group The Orions specialized in performing tunes from the 1950s and 1960s, the heyday of male vocal groups, when acts like The Temptations and Frankie Lymon and the Teenagers ruled the record charts. Although The Orions released some recorded music, they were mostly known for their live performances in and around New York City. Little Joey learned most of The Orions' repertoire by heart and liked to sing along at their shows. Sometimes his brother and sister would join in too.

Obviously, Joseph Sr.'s love of the arts has rubbed off on his family, because Joey is not the only one making a living as a performer today. His sister Janine still sings, while his brother Steven is a dancer with a group called Solid Harmonie and performs at Universal Studios theme park. Even their mother Phyllis has her niche in the world of entertainment. She works at Orlando's famous Sea World aquarium and amusement park.

The Play's The Thing

Around the time Joey turned 13, the Fatone family decided they needed a change of pace. Their Brooklyn district was changing for the worse and they were tired of northeast America's long cold winters. Orlando with its year-round sunshine, lower crime rate and cheaper housing prices seemed like the right solution.

Once there, Joey enrolled in Dr. Phillips High School, which offered an extensive performing arts curriculum. He joined the school chorus and learned to read music by sight. In just a few

weeks his quick progress had so impressed his teacher that Joey was promoted to Chorus II classes, something that was almost never done! Joey was completely in his element. When the time for the school musical came around he auditioned for and won the role of Chino in *West Side Story*. His character didn't have many lines, but Joey was proud because new high school boys didn't normally win speaking parts in the show at all!

Joey's dance skills began to improve as he got involved in school musicals. He had always loved dancing, even way back at the parties he used to go to in his younger days but at Dr. Phillips High School he began to take proper lessons as a dancer. "There I started learning how to actually dance," he said. "I did jazz, modern and stuff like that." He even took tap lessons. In the course of his high school career, Joey performed in a wide variety of plays including more musicals like *Music Man* and *Damn Yankees*, as well as classics such as *Cyrano de Bergerac*, *Macbeth* and *The Merchant of Venice*.

In high school, Joey became friends with JC Chasez through hanging out with some of the *Mickey Mouse Club* members who also went to Dr. Phillips. Joey was the first person JC met in Orlando who wasn't a member of *MMC*. These friends often went to the same parties and even flirted with the same girls some nights! It was the beginning of a friendship that would span the years and benefit both of them later on.

Although Joey and JC both ended up singing together in 'N Sync, that wasn't the first group that Joey was a part of. As a high school senior he was a member of another harmony group called The Big Guys. The four boys in the group – Joey and his friends Eric, Joel and Fonzie – sang at parties, talent shows and school gigs. For a while they even became locally famous stars of the high school set. But it was hard to keep The Big Guys together as high-school graduation approached. Though they were talented and worked well together, as soon as the other boys went away to college, their group split up.

Today, Joey's the most famous former member of The Big Guys, but he's not the only one in the music industry. His old friend Luis Fonzie – once a core member of Joey's school group – is recording songs in Spanish for Universal/Latin Records.

> ## "I started learning how to actually dance…I did jazz, modern and stuff like that."

Monster Mash

When he was still in high school, Joey started doing the rounds of auditions as an actor, dancer and singer. He won small film roles in the organized crime drama *Once Upon A Time In America* and *Matinee*, a spoof of 1950s teen horror flicks starring Kellie Martin. On television, Joey scored a guest-starring role on the science fiction television series *seaQuest DSV*.

While the acting roles were more prestigious, Joey's ability to dance and sing earned him a steady job at Universal Studios Florida theme park. Though he was under eighteen, the park hired him on account of his enthusiasm and talent. As part of the *Beetlejuice Graveyard Review* Joey performed rock music dressed up as famous old time movie monsters like the Wolfman, Dracula or the Phantom of the Opera depending on the show's changing schedule. No matter which monster he played, it was impossible to recognize him under all the special effects makeup! Still, Joey really loved the songs, the silly dance moves, the interaction with the audience and especially the applause. It was an extremely enjoyable and valuable experience for him.

These days, performing at Universal Studios Theme Park remains something of a Fatone family tradition. Joey's brother and sister still work there while they await their own big break into show business!

Universal Studios was where Joey met Chris Kirkpatrick. Immediately, the guys recognized that they shared a lot of similar characteristics. Both loved pretty girls, dancing, nightclubs and dumb jokes. They also shared an appreciation of 1950s vocal groups and a dedication to making it in the music business. When Chris decided to start his own vocal group, it was only logical that he should invite Joey to join.

Joey's light-up-the-room smile and easy-going nature have become invaluable to 'N Sync. Although he doesn't clown around as much as Chris, he's quite a wise guy who enjoys playing practical jokes and making people laugh. He can't bear to see people looking unhappy around him! He's the 'N Sync member most likely to cheer up the others when they're grumpy from a long day on the road or an early start. Once he starts quoting the characters from *South Park* (the cartoon show the boys unanimously like best) even the crabbiest member of the group can't help but grin and join the fun. No matter how tired this brown-eyed performer is, he's perpetually cheerful, armed with a ready smile and an easy laugh.

That's Joey, a guy with personality to spare! He has a knack for easy conversation and he's almost never shy. Happily, Joey's warm nature is a trait he shares freely with 'N Sync's many fans. He's the member of the group most likely to stop and sign one more autograph – even if he risks being late for an appointment. Joey hates to see anyone unhappy, so he really has a hard time saying no, especially if the request comes from a pretty member of the opposite sex! After all, there's a reason that the other guys in the band have christened him 'N Sync's biggest flirt. That's because Joey has never met a woman he doesn't like! Flirting, for Joey, is as natural as breathing and completely unconscious. He can't help but turn on the charm equally for an eight-year-old fan *and* her elderly grandmother!

To his sorrow, lots of girls don't take his interest in them seriously because of his tendency to be flirtatious. It's been said that when 'N Sync performed on the Miss Teen USA pageant, Joey spent an entire night handing out his name and phone number to the 51 contestants but didn't score a single date! Possibly it's a blessing because it would be impossible for Joey to have a steady girlfriend in his life right now.

He had his first romantic relationship with a girl named Jenny from his old Brooklyn neighborhood when he was just ten years old. The same year, he kissed a girl named Lisa when the two of them were pushed into a dark closet together. He's admitted that it wasn't the most wonderful kiss because neither of them knew what to do! Still, it didn't hurt their friendship. Joey still sees Lisa when he goes back to Brooklyn to visit his friends and family. Joey's first date was a more traumatic experience. Aged 13, he took a girl he really liked to see a movie. Though he bought her popcorn and a drink, she never went out with him again!

Just as he's done all his life, Joey also acts as 'N Sync's social director. This friendly guy has no trouble walking up to other performers, saying hi and making arrangements to meet up later on. Some of his famous friends include the guys from the group No Mercy, Nick Lachey of 98° and Lene Crawford Nystrom of Aqua.

He's Super

Joey is proud to proclaim that he's nuts for Superman. The comic book Man of Steel has been his hero since he was just a little child. He collects everything related to Superman, from shirts, books and toys to unique one-of-a-kind items. The collector's edition Superman watch his parents gave him for Christmas a few years ago is one of his most cherished possessions. He's also very proud of some of the early first edition *Superman* comic books that he owns. He wears a jewel-encrusted Superman logo on a necklace, a Superman belt buckle, and even has a tiny Superman tattoo on his right ankle!

Since joining 'N Sync and becoming famous, Joey's Superman collection has tripled in size thanks to generous gifts from his fans. No matter how many toys and collectables he receives, he treats every piece of his collection as a precious item. In his

family's recreation room – which used to be the garage – Joey's Superman memorabilia is neatly arranged on shelves and wrapped in plastic for protection.

Of all the *Superman* gifts he's received, nothing compares to the unique hand-knitted sweater with the Superman insignia on it. It was the handiwork of a particularly talented 'N Sync fan and it took her two months to create! Joey is so thrilled with this great sweater that he's almost afraid to wear it.

One of Joey's dreams is that he will star in a future film version of the Superman story! He'd love to get back into acting – a sentiment his father echoes. He thinks Joey Jr. really has the right stuff for dramatic roles. And playing Superman would be Joey's ultimate dream come true. Although he's heard the news that Hollywood is planning a new *Superman* film starring actor Nicholas Cage, he's convinced he'd be a much better choice for

"Everywhere we go the fans are great."

the role. He's said that all he needs is a few more workouts a week to match Superman's muscle-bound physique!

Joey doesn't only collect Superman paraphernalia. He also likes to bring back souvenir shot glasses from the places he's visited around the world. His collection includes glasses from Hard Rock Cafe and Planet Hollywood restaurants in Europe, South Africa, Asia and America. It's his way of taking home a little tiny piece of the places he's toured.

For Joey, meeting so many people from other cultures is one of the most wonderful perks of his job with 'N Sync. He has said that each place he's visited holds special memories for him, like swimming off the coast of Texas, munching on deep dish pizza in Chicago and going back to visit old friends in New York. In Europe, Joey was knocked out by the architecture of the cities he visited in Germany. Asia was amazing because it was just so different from the west. The beauty of the landscape and the friendliness of the people in South Africa thrilled Joey and the whole group. As for the fans, whether they're speaking English or Japanese, German or Swahili, their love of music has been the universal language. "Everywhere we go the fans are great," Joey remarked.

A real fan of photography, Joey has hours and hours of videotape of 'N Sync's adventures around the world. He likes to use a still camera too. He often chats with the photographer during 'N Sync photo shoots to learn more about the craft of photography. Some day, he'd like to have a darkroom in his own house.

One of the reasons Joey enjoys taking photos so much is that he knows that when he gets home to Orlando, his family will all be eager to see them! Joey's parents and brother and sister remain his biggest supporters and fans. In fact, his mother Phyllis still oversees the handling of 'N Sync's mail for their official fan club. No matter how famous their youngest child gets, he'll still be their little boy. And Joey wouldn't have it any other way. He calls his folks daily on tour and has often flown them out to join him as 'N Sync move around the United States, Mexico, Europe and Canada.

As for the future, Joey predicts that he'll be circling the world at least a dozen more times as a member of 'N Sync. He wouldn't mind doing some acting, too, either with the other guys in a comedy or by himself in a drama. Even if he never gets really to fly like Superman, the dreams that have come true with 'N Sync have already allowed him to soar to the skies!

Joey's Confidential File

THE FACTS

* **Name:** Joseph Anthony Fatone, Jr.

* **Nicknames:** Phat-1, Superman, Party Animal

* **Birth Date:** 28 January 1977

* **Birthplace:** Brooklyn, New York

* **Hometown:** Orlando, Florida

* **Height and Weight:** 6ft tall, 175lb

* **Hair and Eyes:** Brown and brown

* **Parents:** Phyllis and Joseph Fatone, Sr.

* **Brother and Sister:** Steven and Janine

* **Religion:** Catholic

* **Car:** Acura SLX in metallic blue/green

* **Shoe Size:** 12

* **First Kiss:** Lisa, aged ten

* **Unique Collection:** Superman toys

JOEY'S LOVES

* **Music:** Boyz II Men, Mariah Carey, Frankie Lymon and the Teenagers
* **Actors:** Robert De Niro, Sandra Bullock
* **Film:** *Willie Wonka and the Chocolate Factory*
* **Celebrity Crush:** Jenny McCarthy
* **TV Show:** *South Park*
* ***South Park* Character:** Kenny
* **Video Game:** *Bug*
* **Food:** Anything Italian, preferably cooked by mother Phyllis
* **Cereal:** Count Chocula and Sugar Pops
* **Ice Cream:** Mint chocolate chip
* **Candy:** Whatchamacallits
* **Book:** *Macbeth*
* **Treat:** Hot baths!
* **Cologne:** Nicole Miller
* **Walt Disney World Ride:** Tower of Terror
* **Sports Team:** Orlando Magic
* **Place To Visit:** South Africa
* **Gift From A Fan:** A Superman sweater knitted by a German fan
* **Joey's Advice:** "Always try your best."

The Future!

After a brief holiday home with their families, 'N Sync went back into action to ensure that 1999 would be an even greater success for them than 1998. With new music filling their heads and plans for a bigger, better and more elaborate world tour for 1999, the boys had plenty to do!

The experience of opening for Janet Jackson and guesting at radio station Z100's Jingle Ball in New York in December 1998 – a show performed before a sold-out crowd at world-famous Madison Square Garden – gave them lots of ideas about how to approach their own upcoming arena tour. Certainly they planned to bring more of everything to their new show – more music, more costume changes, a bigger stage, flashier lights and more pyrotechnics. They also wanted to find a way to reach out to everyone from the kids in the front row to those in the farthest corners of the arena. It's that connection with their audience – the intimacy of singing along to a song live with your pin-up artist – which they were mindful not to lose.

'N Sync and their advisors created a new stage with a full range of video screens so that no matter where fans were sitting they would never miss a moment of the action on stage. Following the example of other young groups like Hanson, they scheduled a special "meet and greet" time for lucky fan club members into every stop on their spring itinerary. Finally, 'N Sync planned some special surprises for their shows that each night would enable a few lucky fans to get up close on stage with her perfect 'N Sync boy.

In addition to hits like "Tearin' Up My Heart," "I Want You Back" and "(God Must Have Spent) A Little More Time On You,"

the audience at 'N Sync's 1999 arena shows were treated to some of the new songs from the group's third CD. Mostly recorded in February 1999 at Trans Continental Record's new music studio in Orlando, it features a familiar blend of romantic ballads and upbeat dance tracks that are just right for a party. Don't expect 'N Sync to change their sound or write about depressing topics. 'N Sync will always be about having fun.

Once again, the group has harnessed the talents of producers such as Full Force and Max Martin. They also took more charge in the studio. Several of the songs on their newest CD were produced or written in part by the members of 'N Sync. The group also worked harder on perfecting their vocal arrangement on the new songs. As they've worked together and sung together, they've discovered the unlimited possibilities in what the blending of their unique voices can do.

Of course, most of the songs on the third CD were written by well-known songwriters or members of the group themselves, but some tunes reached 'N Sync in a more unusual fashion. According to Justin, the boys received songs that they considered recording from fans! Anyone can send the group a demo tape. 'N Sync encourages submissions and promises to give their professional feedback on the songs with the most potential to novice writers.

In preparation for the new album, 'N Sync recorded a song with the R&B group Ginuwine called "Don't Take Your Love Away". It was their first collaboration, but hopefully, not their last. Each of the boys in 'N Sync knows performers he'd like the group to record with sometime in the future. Their dream list includes Celine Dion (Lance's suggestion), Janet Jackson (JC's), A Tribe Called Quest (Chris's) and Lauryn Hill (Justin's) among others.

How does 'N Sync choose the songs which wind up on their album? Well, it's a lot less complicated than one would imagine. According to Justin, all the finished songs are thrown "in a pit" and then the group and their managers vote on the ones they like best. Everyone gets one vote and the majority rules!

The most important factor in choosing the right song for an 'N Sync CD is what the fans will think of it. 'N Sync try to find a balance of romantic ballads, sweet R&B melodies and rousing party songs which are "very different so that it appeals to everyone," explained Lance. His goal for the third album is to expand the group's audience to include more guys and older adults too.

Over the past year and a half, 'N Sync fans have been incredibly supportive of everything the group has done. It is the fans who inspire Chris, Justin, JC, Joey and Lance to get out of bed at 5 AM to sing on a morning TV news show or to brave the cold and rain to appear at the Thanksgiving Day Parade. The fans make 'N Sync want to be the best they possibly can. "Our fans are the best," said Chris. "They're so great because whether we're doing a show or a TV appearance they're just as into it as we are. We love it."

Television and 'N Sync turned out to be a pretty popular pair in 1999! In addition to making the usual rounds of media chat shows, MTV and award events, the guys finally got to make Lance's dream come true. On 8 February 1999, Lance met one of his dream ladies in show business, Rosie O'Donnell, when 'N Sync appeared on her morning talk show. A longtime fan of the comedienne/actress, Lance admitted that their appearance made him think he'd like a talk show of his own some day! "I can see all of us doing a talk show," Lance said during an online interview with 'N Sync fans. "Not in the next two years, because we're so busy, but I think it would be cool to have a show like Rosie has. A cool show just meeting nice cool people."

And an 'N Sync talk show is only the tip of the iceberg! 'N Sync appeared as themselves on American TV in an episode of the UPN's teen comedy *Clueless*. On the show, which was brodcast on 2 March 1999, Joey, Lance, Justin, JC and Chris show up as guests at Cher's birthday party and serenade the lucky birthday girl with a special rendition of their hit "Tearin' Up My Heart".

The guys also appeared on Melissa Joan Hart's hit Friday night series *Sabrina, The Teenage Witch* in 1999. The members of 'N Sync had a blast playing themselves! On *Sabrina*, their episode was called "Pirate Story." In it, Sabrina and her best friend Valerie, played by perky Lindsay Sloan, are desperate to attend 'N Sync's upcoming concert in their town. Unfortunately, Sabrina's aunts stand in her way when they decide that she is too young to go to the show alone. Could a little magic save the day and give the teenage witch and her pal a chance to meet Joey, Lance, Justin, JC and Chris? You know it!

The members of the group enjoyed their TV appearances so much that a permanent home for 'N Sync on one of the television networks isn't out of the question. Even Lance, the member of the group with the least professional acting experience, admits that being an actor has been one of his dreams since childhood. It looks like he and the rest of 'N Sync might get their chance too. One of the many television projects the group is mulling is a pilot episode written by television producer and former *CHiPs* star Larry Wilcox. The series is visualized as a sort of updated version of *The Monkees* with the members of 'N Sync playing themselves. 'N Sync and Larry, who earned a legion of devoted female fans during the 1970s with his role as a sexy California Highway Patrol motorbike cop, could be the perfect match. The former TV star definitely knows a little something about being a teen idol!

Then there are the movies. After the success of the Spice Girls' 1998 film *Spice World*, Hollywood producers have approached just about every popular and attractive young vocal group making hit music today. 'N Sync is no exception, although the group's members plan to proceed with caution. One script they're considering would place them in the middle of an action/adventure story, an idea that's sure to appeal to a martial arts fan like Chris. The group has also received an offer to star in a comedy film set on a college campus where they would play characters other than themselves. Although nothing's been signed, Justin, Chris, Lance, JC and Joey could begin filming their first movie as early as the summer of 1999!

"...it's been incredible how much everyone has accepted us."

While most of the work they do and the appearances they make are undertaken to promote their band, 'N Sync have always quietly participated in projects to help others. They've frequently given their time to occasions like MTV's annual Rock 'N Jock fundraising events and in 1998 they performed for free at Orlando Bands Together, a multi-act concert to raise money for the victims of the tornadoes which struck central Florida that year. In 1998, 'N Sync also raised their voices along with Backstreet Boys, Aaron Carter and others on a single called "Let The Music Heal Your Soul." Written by Alex Christensen and Frank Peterson, the song was released by Edel America Records to raise funds for the Norduff-Robbins Music Therapy Foundation, a charity that uses music to help treat autistic and severely disabled children. The participating performers released the single as the Bravo All-Stars and scored Top Ten hits in Germany, Norway, Spain and Switzerland. Count on the boys of 'N Sync to continue to support more charity organizations in the future.

'N Sync doesn't anticipate that the Bravo All-Stars project will be the last time they work with Backstreet Boys either. Up until recently, the two groups shared the same management and both

bands still retain ties to Trans Continental head man Louis Pearlman. The members of 'N Sync and Backstreet Boys are friends who are happy to see each other when they meet at industry functions. Both groups claim that their rivalry is more of a creation of the media rather than a real battle of the bands. It's not something that either group wastes a lot of time thinking about.

For 'N Sync, it has been a long, slow climb out of the shadow of Orlando's first five-man pop group. They've succeeded beyond their wildest dreams and proved that there's enough room at the top for two groups from central Florida. Justin, Joey, Lance, Chris and JC are thrilled with how receptive their fans have been. "It's been crazy," said Lance. "We've barely been out a year and it's been incredible how much everyone has accepted us."

'N Sync fans have a lot to look forward to in the coming years too. The boys know that they're only at the beginning of their careers. More music and even bigger and better concert tours are a certainty in their future, with films, television and even their own talk shows all parts of the dream. "For the most part, I think we are really focused on business," explained Justin. "We're very business minded. We're just going from one step to the next."

Wherever the road takes them, Justin, Lance, Joey, JC and Chris plan to be together as 'N Sync for a long, long time. "Nobody wants to be a flash in the pan," explains JC. "People want to create a real career for themselves. And since we're still growing as a group, it's really fun."

'N Sync Confidential Facts!

* When 'N Sync met psychic Uri Geller in the UK, he suggested that if they put a star on the cover of their first CD, it would be a hit. They did and it was!

* The night they learned they'd gone platinum, the members of 'N Sync visited a tattoo shop in Toronto, Canada. Everyone in the group got a tattoo of flames (taken from the design on the "I Want You Back" single cover) except for JC. He's terrified of needles.

* Boxers or briefs? All the guys in 'N Sync actually prefer designer boxer-briefs by Calvin Klein and Tommy Hilfiger.

* Chris carries two good-luck charms. They are a tiny cross and a Native American shield decorated with a bear claw design.

* Justin is the crankiest member of 'N Sync in the morning. He rarely speaks before breakfast.

* Chris already has his next tattoo planned. It will be a dragon which will take up residence on the back of his left leg.

* JC says that the weirdest story that he ever heard about himself was that he was engaged to *Charmed* actress Alyssa Milano. He's never even met her!

* 'N Sync is a democracy. Majority rules in all group decisions. "It's good because we have an odd amount of people," noted Justin.

* Chris owns an enormous collection of vinyl records. In his opinion, the best cities to buy vinyl are New York, Los Angeles and San Francisco.

* 'N Sync's hit CD *Home for Christmas* was recorded in a breakneck four weeks!

* "Here We Go" was picked to be the theme song for the National Basketball Association, but a strike delayed the '98-'99 season!

* It takes about two weeks of twelve-hour-a-day rehearsals to prepare for a new concert tour.

* Ever since Joey said that his wildest fantasy involves a pool of Jell-O, fans have been sending him boxes of the stuff.

* On their last concert tour, 'N Sync used giant water guns to hose down the first ten rows of the audience during their encore.

* All the other guys agree that Joey does not know how to tell a joke right!

* Lance's scariest moment occurred when he was tricked into fighting a real live bull in Cancun, Mexico.

* Though they're starting to like designer labels, all the guys in 'N Sync spend a lot of time shopping for clothing at the US chain of clothing stores, Abercrombie & Fitch.

US Discography

Singles

"I Want You Back"

Released March 1998

Highest US Chart Position: 13

"Tearin' Up My Heart"

Released July 1998

Highest US Chart Position: 5

"Merry Christmas, Happy Holidays"

Released November 1998

Highest US Chart Position: 37

"(God Must Have Spent) A Little More Time On You"

Released November 1998

Highest US Chart Position: 23

Albums

'N Sync

Released April 1998

Highest US Chart Position: 2

Tearin' Up My Heart/I Just Wanna Be With You/Here We Go/For The Girl Who Has Everything/(God Must Have Spent) A Little More Time On You/You Got It/ I Need Love/I Want You Back/Everything I Own/I Drive Myself Crazy/Crazy For You/Sailing/Giddy Up

Home For Christmas

Released November 1998

Highest US Chart Position: 7

Home For Christmas/Under My Tree/I Never Knew The Meaning Of Christmas/Merry Christmas, Happy Holidays/The Christmas Song (Chestnuts Roasting)/I Guess It's Christmas Time/All I Want Is You This Christmas/The First Noel/In Love On Christmas/It's Christmas/Oh Holy Night (A Cappella)/Love's In Our Hearts On Christmas Day/The Only Gift/Kiss Me At Midnight

Video

'N Sync: `N The Mix

The Official Home Video

Released November 1998

Highest US Chart Position: 1

I Want You Back/Tearin' Up My Heart/For The Girl Who Has
Everything/Here We Go/(God Must Have Spent) A Little More Time
On You/Merry Christmas, Happy Holidays

Where to write:

'N Sync Fan Club

PO Box 692109

Orlando, FL 32869-2109

USA

Or visit them on the Web at: www.nsync.com

Acknowledgments

Many thanks to Lance Bass, Chris Kirkpatrick, JC Chasez, Joey Fatone and Justin Timberlake for being such fun interview subjects and the folks at RCA and Trans Continental records for being so knowledgeable and helpful. Huge thanks also go out across the big pond to my patient and ever-gracious editors at Virgin Publishing. Finally, my undying love goes out to my supportive parents, Roseanna and Frank, and always, to Peter.